# GARCÍA LORCA

By Edwin Honig

**A NEW DIRECTIONS PAPERBOOK**

First published clothbound in New Directions' Makers of Modern
Literature Series, 1944
First published paperbound as New Directions Paperbook
Number 102, 1961
Revised edition first published as New Directions Paperbook
Number 102, 1963
Library of Congres Catalog Card Number: 62-12396

*This book is dedicated*
*TO CHARLOTTE*

MANUFACTURED IN THE UNITED STATES OF AMERICA

New Directions Books are published for James Laughlin
by New Directions Publishing Corporation,
333 Sixth Avenue, New York 10014

SECOND PRINTING

# P R E F A C E

LIKE MANY CONTINENTAL WRITERS WHOSE WORKS HAVE
recently come to England and the United States, Federico
García Lorca has been victimized by his enthusiasts.
Those who imported him sought either to make political
capital of his tragic death, or to introduce certain of his
poems as examples of Spanish surrealism. Though both
motives were blameless in themselves, they served to
obscure, when they did not abuse, the poet's art by
misrepresentation. Lorca [1] was neither a "political" nor
a "surrealist" poet—in whatever sense these terms are
used nowadays. He was, however, a *popular* poet in that
special sense reserved to Spain: a poet whose work is
loved and acclaimed by the illiterate and the sophisticated alike for those immediately discernible characteristics through which the Spanish people identify them-

---

[1] In Spanish the surname is customarily given as a composite of
father's name and mother's maiden name in that order. Thus in
Spain or Latin America, the poet is always called García Lorca.
But since Lorca is known to readers of English exclusively by the
second part of his surname, I have followed the English rather than
the Spanish practice throughout.

selves. And he was a *difficult* poet, in the modern phrase, because he attempted to create a personal idiom by relating his understanding of a folk world with the values of an industrial world. In this attempt, he adapted materials and techniques from sources as remote as the medieval Arabic poets and as recent as Breton and Dalí. Yet to recognize his poetry alone is to omit his important dramatic work, for which poetry was, in one sense, a preparation. Poetic and dramatic both, his genius grew not out of advance-guard literary or political movements, but out of a richly functioning Spanish tradition barely surveyed by most present-day criticism. To approach him as an artist at all, one must realize the extent of his integration with that tradition, and understand the kind of sensibility able to thrive so well within it. Thus, in bringing Lorca's art to a focus, the following chapters will stress just such a double projection of traditional use and sensibility.

*       *       *       *

So ran the beginning of the Preface to the first edition of this book in 1944. There have since been certain changes to modify the picture presented there, and even what remains unchanged must now be brought in line with new Lorca information. But the kind of full-scale appraisal that is called for is not the job of this book, originally intended for the non-Spanish reader to whom Lorca was a new name in need of being located. Now as before, the exploration of particulars and work in depth are for others to do. As certain entries in the new Bibliography indicate, such work has been going on, though not enough of it is as solid or as comprehensive as one could expect twenty-five years after Lorca's death. But if their progress has been slow, scholars and critics are not always wholly to blame, for reasons which will shortly emerge.

First, what changes have occurred in the past seventeen years? As Lorca's posthumous fame increases, the glint of political martyrdom, though still apparent, no longer dominates the picture. His plays are now performed almost everywhere, even recently in Spain itself. (There, for the first time since his murder in 1936, a dramatic work of his, *Yerma*, was produced in November, 1960.) He is required reading in hundreds of college courses. With Picasso's and Dalí's his is one of the best-known of twentieth-century Spanish names. The new Aguilar edition of his complete works, a single leather-bound volume in the same format with Cervantes, Calderón de la Barca, and Lope de Vega, has made him a classic author. Perhaps the best sign that his reputation is secure is that some critics have begun to question his ascendancy over the five or six foremost Spanish writers of the period. It is true that Unamuno is still insufficiently recognized outside of Spain; Juan Ramón Jiménez, suddenly honored with a Nobel Prize (in a citation which mentioned Lorca) the year before he died in Puerto Rico, is even less known abroad, though frequently acknowledged to be the greatest poet of his time and Lorca's master. Undeserved obscurity also hangs over Antonio Machado, not to mention Lorca's immediate contemporaries, Jorge Guillén and Pedro Salinas. Whatever the degree of Lorca's greatness, his fame must eventually cause their works to be better known. For it will be impossible to estimate his *oeuvre* without doing justice to theirs, since they all shared in creating the richest literature in Spain since the seventeenth century.

Lorca's masterwork, *The House of Bernarda Alba,* first published in 1946, can now be seen as the climax of his most productive period as a writer, the last five years of his life. The plays *Blood Wedding, Yerma, Doña Rosita the Spinster,* and the poetic works *The Lament for Ignacio Sánchez Mejías* and *The Divan at the Tamarit* all belong to this period. Yet there is more, possibly a good deal more, that has not yet been published—though how much unpublished Lorca material exists or has already been destroyed nobody can say with certainty.

Lorca himself spoke of having written a five-act play called *El público* (*The Audience*). In 1941, and again in 1952, Ángel del Río reported that the play had been completed. Yet during his lifetime the poet permitted only two scenes to be printed in an obscure magazine. Full of irascible vitality, of contentious vengeful sentiment, these fragments excite and confound expectancy by the enormous promise they reveal. They partake of the brilliant mystagogic vision of *Poet in New York,* having been written within a few months of those poems in 1930. In one scene a desperate, virulent exchange between a Figure of the Vine and a Figure of Bells reminds one strongly of Beckett's later play, *Waiting for Godot,* which it exceeds in power. Surely anyone's wanting to withhold this play would be grossly inexcusable and an injustice to Lorca's spirit and genius, which were nothing if not openhanded and free.

# PREFACE

Of *La Destrucción de Sodoma* (*The Destruction of Sodom*), the play Lorca reported as "almost finished" in 1936, no trace exists. Nor do we know whether this title refers to "the mystery play" he mentioned in a Buenos Aires interview in 1934—"I have it in my suitcase." Nor do we know anything about "his last play, *The Dreams of My Cousin Aurelia*, of which"—as his brother Francisco wrote in 1947—"the leading character is Federico himself as a child." Similarly still unlocated is *La Niña que Riega la Albahaca y el Príncipe Preguntón* (*The Girl Who Waters the Sweet Basil Flower and the Inquisitive Prince*), a puppet play produced in Granada on January 5, 1923. *El Sacrificio de Ifigénia* (*Iphigenia's Sacrifice*), presumably begun in 1927, and *La Hermosa* (*The Beauty*), which Lorca called his "political tragedy," are titles of plays which may or may not exist. His last book of poems, *Sonetos del Amor Oscuro* (*Sonnets of Dark Love*), though reported to have been read aloud to his fellow poets Luis Cernuda and Vicente Aleixandre, has not yet come to light. Four of the sonnets (but even their association with the book is not established) have been printed in the Aguilar edition of his complete works.

Of additional Lorca material made available since 1944 and now included in the latest (1960) Aguilar edition, there is an incomplete version, in two acts and seven scenes, of *El Maleficio de la Mariposa* (*The Witchery of the Butterfly*), his first play; the salty puppet play in six scenes, *The Tragicomedy of Don Cristóbal and Rosita;* selections from the out-of-print edition of *Impressions and Landscapes,* a travel book

vii

published when Lorca was eighteen; several short prose pieces and dialogues; about a dozen lectures and speeches, including the now famous account of the *duende*. In addition there are represented a scattering of Lorca's letters to friends, the texts of numerous newspaper interviews (collected by Marie la Ffranque), poems from his book of *Suites,* fifteen of his songs and twenty-five of his drawings. And although most of this material is a vital part of the Lorca record, its appearance does not compensate for the still-missing plays and book of sonnets.

Most work on Lorca has been biographical and only incidentally concerned with literary analysis. Friends and acquaintances still clutter the landscape with memorabilia, unconstrained by any impulse to inquire into the complex nature of the man as a human being. No, he must be an idol, a lovable child, a tragic symbol! One exception is Jorge Guillén's warm homage to the memory of their friendship in the later 1920s. Another is the diplomat Carlos Morla's diaries (1926–1936); urbane and starry-eyed by turns, they still make interesting reading for their accounts of day-to-day events and Lorca's circle of friends. In a category by itself is Jean-Louis Schonberg's exasperating and heavily rationalistic thesis-pushing account of Lorca's disturbed sexuality. In Ángel del Río's intelligent introductory study to *Poet in New York* (see Ben Belitt's bilingual edition, a model of scrupulous textual work and heroic translating), biographical material is scanted in favor of a rather literal reading of the poem's structure and the historical circumstance of its genesis. Even so, Professor del Río avoids the bad manners and ineptness of so much "appreciative" Lorca criticism which drowns out the text with resounding displays of the commentators' personal fireworks. Few Lorca critics have shown the skill to pass effectively across the dim border between biographical and contextual criticism. Perhaps this is due to the uncharted and unformulated condition of available information about their subject. But even when such an effort is made and new biographical information is introduced, as in Schonberg's book, we get a tendentious and dithyrambic scramble of the critic's own prepossessions.

What one encounters then, in highly fragmented form so far, are three types of accounts. The first is written by Lorca's literary friends, none of them very close observers, who tend to play up the poet's magnetic charm and personal showmanship—the mask and not the man. The second are the accounts of distant acquaintances or friends of friends, who magnify the traffic of hearsay and fabricate personality theories or social and political sermons out of them. The third are the reports of friends who suppress more than they reveal of Lorca's life and works. Meanwhile the appearance of a handful of Lorca's letters, newspaper interviews, and radio talks gives one unexpected side-views of the poet's response to fame and his sense of mission. But since this material is still unevaluated and fragmentary, the picture often slips out of focus and becomes paradoxical; then we see the private nature of Lorca's personality emerging in public utterances while the public (masklike) features crop up in intimate exchanges with friends.

Unlike Yeats, Lorca had no set poetic system; unlike Eliot, his poetry and plays show no line of religious or ideological development. And if a good deal of his early work (in *Libro de Poemas, Canciones* and *El Maleficio de la Mariposa*) is nurtured by Jiménez' exquisitism, Lorca never perfected the older poet's glittering style of expression, perhaps because he could not be contained by the kind of arduously cultivated objective perceptivity it required. Lorca was more like Unamuno and Dylan Thomas: a self-dramatist possessed by the effort to describe the conflict of natural forms seeking escape from death and thereby lighting up the intensest of living moments. And so behind the mask of the gypsy in *Romancero Gitano* and of the Negro in *Poeta en Nueva York*, Lorca succeeded in being more personal than in the subjective lyricism of *Canciones*. In the same way, his *Lament* for the bullfighter is perhaps more intensely Spanish than his strongly honor-ridden plays about women. We should expect of a poet whose temperament is dramatic an acutely personal way of speaking that is not at the same time merely confessional. And similarly, of someone possessed by the idea of capturing reality in the conflicting flashes of the moment, we should expect a gradual discarding of ornament, poetic ritual and symbolism for the barest, most essential kind of prose, such as we find in *The House of Bernarda Alba*.

Some of these matters have been held up to systematic

scrutiny—as, for example, the mythical complex of Lorca's art in a Cassirer-derived exegesis by Gustavo Correa, and the metaphysics of Lorca's "intensity" in a study by Christoph Eich, largely founded on the theories of Bergson and Bachelard. Under pressure of their system-making, these studies mistake the product of thought for the process of atavistic expression and revelation which is the poetry itself. To such highfalutin analyses one prefers a sober descriptive survey of Lorca's work, such as Díaz-Plaja's, or Berenguer Carisomo's early, sensitive account of Lorca's temperament as seen through the poet's special use of themes, or Arturo Barea's warmly informative estimate of "the poet and his people" in what is, incidentally, the most thoroughly readable book on the poet to date.

Yet none of these studies has much to say about the fundamental fact that there is something in Lorca's later plays and poems which perplexes us. (And let us remember that *When Five Years Pass, Bernarda Alba,* and *Poet in New York* were not finally seen through the press by the poet himself.) Our perplexity results from an unfulfilled promise in the work—the accumulation of a force that was just beginning to find new expressive forms. This was being poured into those works and projects of the last few years of his life, furiously, breathlessly, and yet with a strangely deliberate clarity, as though he were aware that there might not be time to finish any of them. "It happens with me that three or four years go by in mulling over a play and then I write it down in a fortnight," he told a reporter in 1935. This may have been a favorite way of propitiating the fates, of overcoming the inevitable with the imposition upon it of the inconceivable, the unachievable work. Or it may just have been a statement of fact about a way of working. Still, in view of what we know about the power of dramatic statement in *Bernarda Alba*, the two scenes of *The Audience*, and the later poems, we can say that what disturbs us are the signs, the first stirrings, of a new dramatic language, even a new dramatic orientation, based on a necessity of the imagination to break through the impasse of sterility, already so insistently documented in his last three plays.

Somewhere in a letter to Jorge Guillén, Lorca wrote that poetry is made out of love, force, and renunciation. The statement tells us something about the springs of his personality; it also says much about his literary procedures, his themes, and his problematical forcing of the door of the constant enemy, death. For what are these three paradoxical elements but a synthetic figure for human pride—a figure which attempts to assert the meaning of life against death? This is what Mariana Pineda stands for: in the end her triumphant love, her struggle to make it pervade her action, her self-sacrifice, and through this, her powerless fight against martyrdom and its dehumanizing consequence of being turned into an abstraction. The triple complex of love-force-renunciation appears in the "erotic aleluya" *Don Perlimplín*, in *Yerma*, in *Blood Wedding*, in a more diffuse form in *Bernarda Alba*, as a fight against sterility, false honor (the tyranny of "whiteness") which is both chastity and death. Human pride is the ability to declare through a course of self-sacrifice what human love, however misunderstood, must affirm in the teeth of death and its own destruction. The figure of human pride is present in the gypsy's contention against the weapons of the law, in his erotic code, and in his last disdainful encounter with death. It is also present in the ever-new, ever-repeated encounter between the bullfighter and the bull, which must end in death, and, if fought well, in glory.

Reality, Lorca said, is prose, what lives now, the present tense: *it is*. The beauty of truth is poetry, timeless, always existent, all tenses. To be made conceivable, reality requires the poet's strategy, and poetry needs for its truth what Lorca called "the opening of the veins"—the expression of human pride in love, force, and renunciation. Understood in this way, Lorca at the end of his life was writing for very high stakes—and the only ones by which he could sustain his vision of human pride. "When the pure forms were wiped out," he ends a poem in *Poet in New York,*

> . . . I sensed that they had murdered me.
> They swept through cafés, graveyards, churches,
> they opened the wine casks and the closets,
> they ravaged three skeletons to yank the gold teeth out.
> But they never found me.
> They never found me?
> No. They never found me.

The lines have often been taken as a prophecy of his own death in the Goyesque horrors of the Spanish Civil War. But they speak more precisely about his obsession with the figure of human pride. They say that in a world where the possibility of the triple human equation no longer exists, there is only murder and pillage, death and anonymity. If we have anything to learn by studying

Lorca, it is, in the end, the knowledge of how he attempted to uphold the pure forms, the strategies of victory against certain defeat in the arena of every day, the life of uncontestable reality.

*    *    *    *

For biographical material I am indebted to Martínez Nadal's introduction to Spender's translations of Lorca's *Poems* (1939) and to Ángel del Río's study of the poet, *Vida y Obras de Federico García Lorca* (1941 and 1952). However, all the translations which appear in the following pages are, for better or worse, my own. Others to whom acknowledgments are due are: Professor Nicholson B. Adams, in whose seminar class long ago the idea for this book found its first expression; the late Professor Joaquín Ortega, "a Spanish island" in himself, to whom I owe my awakening to the Spanish literary genius; Ángel Flores for his description of Lorca's New York visit; and the editors of *The New Mexico Quarterly* and *Poetry* (Chicago) for permission to use portions of my articles which first appeared in those magazines.

Lafayette, Indiana, 1943
Albuquerque, New Mexico, 1948
Providence, Rhode Island, 1961

# C O N T E N T S

# CONTENTS

# 1. THE JUGGLER

FEDERICO GARCÍA LORCA WAS BORN IN FUENTEVAQUEROS, Granada, on June 5, 1898. His father, Don Federico García Rodríguez, an energetic and well-to-do farmer, had married as a widower Doña Vicenta Lorca, an intelligent school teacher, and, as her son always insisted, a highly educated and imaginative one. From the beginning, it was she who nurtured his musical and poetic interests. The young Federico was deeply attached to his parents; and they in turn seem to have provided him with the warm sense of home and of love for the land upon which his art and personality increasingly thrived. A childhood ailment prevented him from speaking until he was three, and from walking until he was four. Even long after, he was known to walk with a perceptible limp. The only signs of precocity which suggest his later development as an artist were his ability to learn popular songs at two and, a little later, his enthusiasm for constructing miniature theatres and conducting imaginary church masses. One

1

of his favorite games was to imitate the local priest's fiery sermons. These the boy delivered with rare ardor before the family and house servants, making them promise beforehand to weep bitterly at the conclusion. One servant seems to have pleased him particularly, being sincerely moved by his oratory to weep copiously without invitation or restraint.

His home life was a happy one, and his parents were eager to educate the young Federico to an early understanding of fine literature. He was exposed to most of Victor Hugo and Cervantes, and with the latter's *Don Quijote* he became familiar in its entirety. After a brief attendance at the Colegio del Sagrado Corazón de Jesús in the city of Granada, he enrolled in the University of Granada to undertake studies for a career in law. But Federico was less than a mediocre student, and when he quit the University for the Residencia in Madrid, he was already seeking stimulation from literary men rather than the course of academic honors. Years later, however, he returned to the University of Granada, and for no apparent practical purpose finally took his degree in Law. The period of childhood and adolescence, before he left for Madrid in 1919, determined his development as a poet. His apprenticeship to music and letters in Granada, and Granada itself, an open-air paradise which had been permanently colored by a good part of Western, Mediterranean, and near-Eastern civilization, provided the young Federico with as rich poetic material as could be found anywhere. It was here, while scarcely conscious of the process, that he became intimate with the old cultures: the classic Roman and Greek, the Arab, the Gypsy, and

2

with the superb language and imagery of the seventeenth century Spanish poets. It was here too that he learned to appreciate the nineteenth century nostalgia for lost loves and diminutive gardens. The ancient city of Granada, once the Moorish capital of Spain, lay among warm hills cut by winding millennial streams—a world saturated with the resignation of its provincial inhabitants and with the long wild songs of the gypsies in neighboring caves. The sensual metaphor and the spicy idiom of Andalusian peasantry did not have to be excavated from a lost folk tradition; they were still as alive here in Granada as they had ever been since the Middle Ages.

That all this was to be basic to the poet's mature work, and that he was to gain clarity and stature as he assimilated the traditions of the life and cultures about him, could not be foreseen from his first literary activities. One cannot say what led him so early to his prodigious reading: the nineteenth century Spanish Romantics, the Latin American Modernists and Spanish contemporaries, the French Symbolists, Shakespeare, and the Spanish and Greek classics. It would seem, however, that if he was seeking an apprenticeship to literature, his choices were instinctively sound, as they were also perhaps inevitable for an educated Spanish student. When he patterned his early poems on his favorite authors, he was doing no more than what countless writers have done in their intoxicated and muddled adolescence. From his fifteenth to his eighteenth year, Lorca was writing and reading feverishly, with the counsel of friends and teachers at college. He had learned to play the guitar and the piano with unusual dexterity. One day, in fact, while Lorca was playing some

Beethoven sonatas on the piano, Fernando de los Ríos, President of the Centro Artístico de Granada, was struck by what he believed an extraordinary talent. He became interested in the boy and undertook to guide his development. This proved crucial for the young Lorca; for de los Ríos not only helped direct the poet's early steps, but throughout Lorca's career often provided the incentive for certain decisions which had important consequences for his art.

Lorca soon joined a literary group in Granada, and published his first article there in 1917: a tribute to the poet Zorrilla on the centennial of his birth. As far as I know, no        this publication has turned up; [1] but one can well imagine what Lorca, freshly influenced by the Romantics and an avid devotee of Zorrilla's poetic legends, must have written in his praise on this occasion. The Spaniard's extreme eagerness to commemorate his poets' birthdays is proverbial. Foreigners often look curiously at his annual pilgrimages to the graves of famous precursors, a ceremony affording the Spaniard's national pride an outlet for display. But in addition, the abundant eulogies which follow in all publications great and small permit the young and aspiring not only to pay off their literary debts, but to break into print for the first time. In publishing his homage to Zorrilla, Lorca was following this well-defined practice. Whatever its actual results, the young writer probably gained some measure of confidence in his own literary efforts.

In the following year, as a result of a tour through Spain with a class in the Theory of Literature and Art, Lorca wrote and published a little book, *Impresiones y Paisajes*

4        [1] It appears in *Obras Completas* (Aguilar, 1960).

# THE JUGGLER

(*Impressions and Landscapes*). Unfortunately, this book has long been out of print and is almost impossible to obtain. Martínez Nadal, the Spanish critic and Lorca's friend, points out the importance of this journey for the poet and recalls his saying later, "For the first time I became fully aware of myself as a Spaniard." And this is significant as a reply to criticism of Lorca for his provincialism and exaggerated exploitation of Granada to the exclusion of the rest of Spain.

Prompted by Fernando de los Ríos, who had discerned a new need in Lorca's poetry, the young man, taking with him several copies of his book and a manuscript of poems, quit the University of Granada in 1919 to go to the Residencia de Estudiantes in Madrid. Here at the Residencia, which Martínez Nadal calls "that Spanish interpretation of English college life," the intellectual and artistic center of Spain had been formed. Established as a result of the educational reform movement of 1898, the Residencia offered a liberal arts and science training in the enlightened manner of the best European universities. Its aim was to educate intellectual and social leaders, cosmopolitan in outlook, but with the advancement of a modernized Spain at heart. Attendance at lectures was voluntary, examinations were grouped over wide intervals, and the student was given as broad and as personal a choice in his studies as he could desire. The best teachers of modern Spain had begun to lecture here, including Francisco Giner de los Ríos, the man who had revolutionized higher education and by sheer personality and teaching genius had introduced a renaissance of learning in Spain. Of Giner de los Ríos Salvador de Madariaga has written,

5

"Directly or indirectly, consciously or unconsciously, there is no man who counts in Spanish culture today who has not come under his teachings." If there ever existed a high incentive for formal study, it was here at the Residencia. Yet, characteristically, Lorca remained passive and averse to seizing what many would have considered a rare opportunity for intellectual growth. Seldom attending lectures, and coming under the spell of a new kind of life with new friendships, he finally gave up the idea of taking a certificate in Madrid.

There were other things in Madrid at the end of the First World War to stir an imaginative young man of twenty from the provinces, already conscious of his unusual talents and confident of his future achievement. The creative and revolutionary energies which the war had released in the rest of Europe were beginning to be felt in Spain. Instigated by the Generation of '98—Giner de los Ríos, Pérez Galdós, Unamuno, followed by de Madariaga and Ortega y Gasset—the repudiation of decadent medievalism was now being emphasized through what was happening in Europe. A new sensitivity became manifest again in a Spain which had long kept itself splendidly, if somewhat suicidally, isolated from the rest of the world. But Spain was still primarily an agrarian nation, and had not suffered the embattled experience of Europe. It could indulge in the anarchic and revolutionary movements begun across the Pyrenees without having undergone the disillusionment which had generated them. This activity animated the younger generation, who were spared, however, the fractured vanguardism of the French, for example. To be sure, Spanish versions of cubism and dadaism did spring up. But those who became wholehearted disciples were eventually compelled to emigrate to Paris to find nourishment. The men who stayed evolved their own symbols and techniques, which were respected because they were original and not flea-bitten by the French forms. Even ultraism, a Spanish literary movement designed on much the same principle as English and American imagism and aimed at deflating the reputation of the Spanish Modernists and the school of Rubén Darío, was culturally still-born. It was indicative of his good sense, and of his intuitive understanding of what is basic to the Spanish character, that Lorca did not join his friends in simulating the European post-war literary jitters. This is not to say that he always remained immune to their postures or to their wild metaphoric innovations. Lorca was constantly assimilating almost unnoticeably a valuable store of insight from books, ideologies and practices, while rejecting them as panaceas. This capacity, reflected in both his best and his inferior work, was often to raise the contradictory cries of "surrealist" and "literary provincial" against him. The fact is, however, that more than many of his contemporaries he worked originally and at close quarters with the rich Spanish tradition.

What he shared with his generation was enthusiasm for the work of the already well-established poets like Juan Ramón Jiménez, Antonio and Manuel Machado, and writers like Ramón del Valle-Inclán, Miguel Unamuno and Azorín. These men had proved that they could build a significant contemporary art on the basis of traditional Spanish culture. They were the constant reminders to the young of the enduring greatness of Spain's Middle Age and Renaissance literature. They were admired because they achieved originality without regard for applause from the Madrid middle class or the shifting winds of the great literary movements from the continent. Through a personally contrived artistic discipline, they reinvigorated the habits of a cultural perception established by Cervantes, Lope de Vega, Calderón de la Barca, and traditional balladry. They were the contemporary masters whom Lorca accepted and who later welcomed him among them.

Meanwhile, basking in the light of appreciative comradeship at the Residencia, the young poet did nothing to suggest the arduous private compulsions of a great talent in the making. Perhaps our Northern conception of the pallid ascetic working himself to death, friendless and repudiated in a great city or in the corner of a province, is not always suited to the Latin personality. We may forget that the climate of creative fellowship can be as important to the growing artist as the isolation of a distempered and half-persecuted existence among the "enemy" in a cultural void. This fact is tremendously significant in regard to Lorca. For it explains the spontaneity which saturated all his art. When Lorca found an encouraging audience who would listen to his poems and improvisations for hours at a time, he had no concern for publication. The way of the old troubadours—communication through enactment, through word of mouth—was the more satisfactory. From the time of his beginnings as a lyric poet, he had the urge for dramatic representation that found full expression later in his writing for the

8

theatre. The full flowering of his personality was essential to the growth of his art. Only by satisfying this deep histrionic need—a marked trait in most Spaniards, especially in the demonstrative and creative Andalusian—could he body forth his lively poetic talent. By his musical and poetic recitals, he held a serious intellectual crowd under the same enchantment which a larger theater audience was later to feel on witnessing his plays. Thus the phenomenon arose, rare in contemporary literature, of a new poetic art appearing without the intermediary of publication. As one commentary on Lorca has put it: "Many poems came to him verbally—verbally, because the poet recited them aloud as he conceived and composed them, and at times put off transcribing them, or more often, giving them out for publication. And so, during those years when he still had not published a book and only a handful of poems had appeared in a few new magazines, García Lorca already enjoyed renown in literary circles where his verses passed from mouth to mouth as if they were a tradition." [1]

Except for annual summer sojourns at his home in Granada, Lorca remained at the Residencia until 1928. During this period, finding the friendship and criticism by which he could test himself, he became Spain's most respected young poet. In 1920, his first play, *El Maleficio de la Mariposa* (*The Witchery of the Butterfly*), was staged by Martínez Sierra in Barcelona. This was followed in 1921 by his first book of poems, *Libro de Poemas*. Then, during a visit to his home in 1923, he produced the puppet play, *La Niña Que Riega la Albahaca y el Príncipe Pre-*

[1] Alfredo de la Guardia, *García Lorca: Persona y Creación.*

9

guntón (*The Girl Who Waters the Sweet Basil Flower and the Inquisitive Prince*). Lorca himself designed the sets, and the musical commentary with compositions of Debussy, Ravel, Albéniz and Pedrell was arranged by Manuel de Falla, who also accompanied on the piano. In the same year Lorca began to paint. The exhibition of his paintings in a Barcelona gallery in 1927 indicated an original coloristic imagination, although the conceptions were often crude and hastily performed. He himself made no overt pretenses about them; they were clearly intended as a supplement to his poetical ideas, rather than as an independent contribution in another medium.

His friendship with Salvador Dalí and with the better-known poets among his contemporaries, Jorge Guillén, Rafael Alberti, Pedro Salinas, Gerardo Diego, and Dámaso Alonso, introduced him to certain new currents in esthetic ideas. With Dalí, he found a new stress on the objects of a dream world in surrealist landscapes, and he appreciated at least the literary justice of such representations. But, as he showed later in his *Oda a Salvador Dalí,* Lorca was struck more, perhaps, by the close analogy between the painter's attempt to find a personal pictorial form and his own attempt to find such a form through poetry. In Alberti, Lorca recognized a fellow poet with similar concerns for reworking the old folk ballad into modern poetry. But Salinas, Guillén, and the rest were still experimenting in the top story; they were primarily intellectual poets for whom the direct use of folk themes —the work in the bottom story—was inadequate for shaping their rather strict and depersonalized idioms. Lorca, however, had already written *Canciones* (*Songs*), *Poema del Cante Jondo*) (*Poem of the Deep Song*), and *Romancero Gitano* (*Book of Gypsy Ballads*), though none of these had yet appeared in book form. These volumes were to establish him above all his contemporaries as Spain's most important popular poet. Meanwhile he shared actively in the work of his friends and fellow poets; and when, at the tercentenary of Góngora's death in 1927, a group of them inaugurated a series of lectures at the Residencia to re-valuate Spain's most difficult Golden Age poet, Lorca contributed a paper on "La Imágen Poética de Don Luis de Góngora" ("The Poetic Imagery of Don Luis de Góngora"). That same year, aided by Salvador Dalí, who de-signed the sets, Lorca presented his first full-length play in Madrid, *Mariana Pineda*.

The chronology of Lorca's written work seldom coin-cides with that of his published work. Thus, before he left Spain for New York in 1929, he had a considerable group of manuscripts: some already published, like *Canciones* (1927) and *Romancero Gitano* (1928); others not published until later, like *Poema del Cante Jondo* (1931); some not published until after his death, like the volume of early verse *Primeras Canciones* (1936), and the play *Amor de Don Perlimplín con Belisa en Su Jardín* (*Love of Don Perlimplín for Belisa in His Garden*) (1938); some published only in part after his death, like the book of *Odas* and *Suites;* [1] and the rest still unpublished to date.

The circumstances directly preceding Lorca's sudden decision to leave Spain have been described by Angel del Río:

At the beginning of the year 1929, the author of *Romancero Gitano* is enjoying a full measure of success. His name has already

[1] *Suites* appears in *Obras Completas* (Aguilar, 1960).

become popular. His influence is being felt by other poets. In Granada, a group of young men—Joaquín Amigo, Banús, Francisco Ayala, Fernández Casado, Menoyo—acclaim him as their master and publish the magazine *Gallo* under his inspiration. At a fine lecture given at the Lyceum Club in Madrid on the subject of "Imagination, Inspiration and Evasion in Poetry," he triumphs as a critic and gives proof of another aspect of his many-sided talent. Undoubtedly public flattery awakens his child-like vanity. But inwardly, such demonstrative success leaves him dissatisfied. He undergoes a crisis of disillusionment. The causes are not clear, even to his closest friends. Martínez Nadal, his constant companion in these days, tells us, 'As the months passed by and the popularity of the book (*Romancero*) increased, the poet felt the weight of his own work. This, along with other intimate reasons, made him pass through the only period of depression in his life. He grew sad, isolated himself, said nothing of his plans, and, stranger still, no longer recited his new poems.' Lorca had grown aware of the danger of his success. He knew that many artists had ruined themselves by living on their easy triumphs. He does not recognize himself in the role of gypsy poet which begins to circulate. 'My use of the gypsy,' he would say, 'is intended as a literary theme for a book. Nothing more.' Above all, he is hurt by the less than generous allusions guardedly made among a few pontiffs of the new literature. In these he sees a basis for rivalry which he finds alien to himself. There was also, as Martínez Nadal suggests, some emotional disturbance of his intimate life, to which he would later refer sadly and obscurely. The crisis resolves itself into a desire for flight, and for the first time he seeks to leave Spain.

His destination was decided when he learned that Fernando de los Ríos, his friend and former teacher, was leaving for New York in the summer of 1929. Joining de los Ríos in the passage across, Lorca settled on arrival at Columbia University, where he took a dormitory room in John Jay Hall.

It might be supposed that such a migration would have

serious consequences for one so attached as Lorca to the land of his origin. The experience was indeed tremendous, not simply because it found expression in the most bizarre book of poems he ever wrote (*Poeta en Nueva York*), but because it resulted in the evidences of a spiritual transformation giving new direction to the whole of his art. Whether Lorca came to New York to escape the barren intellectualism of the European spirit that had infiltrated Spain; whether he sought merely to escape from the results of a too easy triumph which came when *Romancero Gitano* was published; whether he sought peace from envious literary rivals who were abusing his name and his intentions; or whether he had a more intimate personal reason for leaving Spain—all or any of these motives were soon forgotten in the maelstrom of the new life he was observing: an existence which he would never have believed possible in his wildest dreams of the tormented gardens he had written about in Spain.

Again, as at the Residencia in Madrid, the warmth of his personality, his ability to create an intimate, joyful atmosphere by his songs and recitals, won him the admiration of a small circle at Columbia University. He soon took for himself the resounding title, "Director of the Mixed Choruses of the Instituto de Las Españas in the United States of America." With characteristic academic insouciance, he enrolled in several English courses, only to withdraw because of impatience and a sense of his linguistic limitations. Even the few English words he learned, he pronounced badly. Joined by several friends, and for a while, by Ignacio Sánchez Mejías, the literary Andalusian bullfighter whose skill in the arena he respected profoundly, Lorca's infectious hilarity suffered no diminution in this new atmosphere. To those who never knew him by reputation or through his own language—the university students, the dormitory telephone operator, the Negro elevator attendants—he became a familiar figure with his laughter, his strange walk, his pirouettes and deep bows. He arranged new songs for La Argentinita, the Spanish dancer, repeated his lecture, "Imagination, Inspiration and Evasion in Poetry," at Columbia, and delivered a new one with musical accompaniment, "The Lullaby in Spanish Poetry," at Vassar College. Fascinated by the Negro, he was constantly drawn to Harlem night life, where the thump of drums and the throaty rhythms of the blues singers excited him in much the same way that the Andalusian gypsy had done in Spain. He wandered through Harlem streets by day and saw into the dark suffering of the crowded houses where the great Negro was "prisoner in a janitor's uniform." He visited Wall Street, walked along the wharves on the Hudson River, measured the Chrysler Building with a "cry against Rome," and strode by night across the Brooklyn Bridge. There was even a short meeting with Hart Crane. Ángel Flores, the New York editor and translator who introduced the two men, remarks that, unfortunately, neither was aware of the other's poetic accomplishment. It was almost as if two transatlantic liners had passed each other without signals in the black of night. The bohemianism of Lorca's dress at the Residencia—flowing tie and black coat—was replaced by a collegiate V-necked sweater much in vogue in America at the time, and a shirt collar loosely enclosed by a tie with an enormous knot. He found

and extravagant stage design. Lorca's fame reached out to
Latin America, and in 1933 he was invited to Buenos
Aires to produce both his own plays and his versions of
the Golden Age dramas. Here a new audience was drawn,
one which had never come to the theater before. At one
performance of Lope de Vega's *La Dama Boba* (*The
Foolish Lady*), approximately sixty thousand persons were
in attendance. Seldom before had a Spaniard been received with such enthusiasm in Latin America. Surrounded by many of the best-known artists during his
several months' sojourn in Buenos Aires, Lorca passed
through a whirl of theatrical performances, lectures and
literary parties. Before his return to Spain, a group representing the South American countries publicly proclaimed
him ambassador of Spanish letters.

Such fanfare might have overwhelmed a man less used
to it than Lorca, and even one indifferent to it. It seems
to have elevated Lorca and prepared him for further accomplishment, which came in Madrid with the productions of his plays *Yerma* and *Doña Rosita la Soltera* in
1935. The same year, in New York, an unsuccessful translation of *Bodas de Sangre* was staged under the strange
title, *Bitter Oleander*. Of the critics, only Stark Young,
writing in the *New Republic*, could see through the thick
curtain of strained English idiom into something of the
original's wild poetic beauty. Meanwhile, Lorca was preparing another group of poems for publication, *El Diván
del Tamarit*, and his *Llanto por Ignacio Sánchez Mejías*
(*Lament for Ignacio Sánchez Mejías*) was being widely
repeated throughout Spain and Latin America. By 1936,
he had finished a new folk tragedy, *La Casa de Bernarda*

**17**

*Alba,* and was at work on another, *La Destrucción de Sodoma,* when the news of the Moorish insurrection reached the capital in July. Refusing invitations to come to Colombia and Mexico, and against the advice of his friends, Lorca returned south that summer, as had been his custom, to his home in Granada.

It was from Granada a few weeks later that the first laconic report was received in Madrid announcing his murder by a Franco firing squad. To those who knew him, the news was as incomprehensible as it was terrifying. Lorca had never espoused a political cause of any kind. He had fled the bickerings of factions with an instinctive dread for all political dogma. He had once jestingly replied to a question calculated to arouse some partisan admission, that he was a Catholic, Communist, Anarchist, Libertarian, Traditionalist and Monarchist all at once; this was simply his way of stating his integrity as a Spaniard. A few months before his death, in an interview published in the Madrid daily, *El Sol,* he was quoted as saying,

I am completely a Spaniard, and it would be impossible for me to live outside of my geographical boundaries; but I hate him who is a Spaniard only to be nothing more. I am a brother to everybody and I despise the man who sacrifices himself for an abstract nationalist idea only to love his country with a bandage over his eyes.

Undoubtedly the Fascist terrorists who killed him had something like these utterances in mind, if not also the belief that Lorca represented the free democracy of popular Spain which they were delivering to Hitler for target practice. Angel del Ríos's reconstruction of the event, as

**18**

gathered from the accounts of various witnesses, describes Lorca as having taken refuge in the home of a friend, a member of the *falangistas,* Franco's youth group. The "authorities" in Granada, taking advantage of his host's momentary absence, entered the house and dragged Lorca away. His friend, later inquiring after him, was told that Lorca had been detained but that he would be released the next day if no charges were offered against him. Obviously, these "charges" must have been found or concocted, for the following morning Lorca gave his life as did thousands of other innocents that day in cities throughout southern Spain.

## 2. HIS HERITAGE

ANY DISCUSSION OF LORCA'S POETRY MUST BEGIN WITH AN
examination of the literary traditions which emerged from
the old hybrid cultures of Spain, particularly in the southern provinces of Andalusia. Before seeking to estimate
the distinctively modern qualities of his poetry, we must
understand his art as primarily an expression of national
genius. The main aspects of the Spanish lyric tradition
which find a new culmination in Lorca's poetry are: the
medieval Arabic-Andalusian art of amorous poetry together with the early popular ballad; the Renaissance synthesis in Spain of the Greco-Latin poetic art, accomplished
by the sophisticated "conceptist" poetry of Luis de Góngora; and the broad body of Andalusian gypsy art known
as *cante jondo*, "deep song."

In eleventh century Andalusia, Arabic poets had already perfected the style of the short lyric called the *casida*. Islam's best imaginative constructions flourished in
the southern part of the Spanish peninsula, and even en-

tered a period of decline before *El Cantar de Mío Cid,* the great Spanish epic, was written. The spirit of the desert, transplanted in the luxuriant Andalusian landscape, introduced a tightly wrought imagery into Spanish lyricism which can be clearly distinguished for centuries up through the present. One facet of Arabic-Andalusian art is its astonishing obsession with erotic love, reinforced by the Platonic notion of chastity. Poetic sensibility aimed at a morbid perpetuation of desire always conditioned by a moral-esthetic idea of sexual purity. Such an attitude towards love had already become popular among Bedouin tribes in the early pre-Islamic period, especially among those of the *Beni-Odra,* "Sons of Virginity." Somewhat later, in the tenth century, the theologian Abenaud of Ispakan made the first poetic systematization of Platonic love in his *Book of the Planet Venus.* This ideal, dominating the Arabic lyric in Andalusia for almost three centuries, caught the imagination of medieval European poetry, into which it entered as a direct inspiration to the *gaya ciencia* of the Provençal school and the *dolce stil nuovo* of the early Italian school of Guido Guinizelli, Dante's master. Here, for example, is the translation of a poem, "Chastity," written by a prominent Arabic poet in 976:

Although she was ready to succumb, I abstained from her and did not obey the temptation offered me by Satan.

Unveiled, she appeared in the night, and the nocturnal darkness, illumined by her face, also raised its veil.

But I realized the divine precept which, condemning lust, is like a chamberlain guarding the portals of my passion, preventing my instinct from rebelling against chastity.

21

And so I passed the night with her like a thirsty little camel whose muzzle prevents him from suckling, or as in a flower garden where, for one like myself, there was no other purpose than to look and to smell.

For I am not like those abandoned beasts who use gardens for pasturage.

And in this vein, another Arabic poet describes "The Storm":

Every flower opened its mouth in the darkness, seeking the udder of fertilizing rain,
and the armies of black clouds, loaded with water, passed majestically in review, like Ethiopian troops, armed with the golden saber of lightning.

Or a twelfth century poet writes of "Insomnia":

When the bird of sleep tried to nest in my eye, he saw my eyelashes and was startled, frightened by nets.

The tendency throughout was to petrify the image, to treat the metaphor according to definite analogies based on the hierarchies found in nature: man compared with animals, animals with flowers, and flowers with precious stones. But unlike the European poet, the Arabic had no temporal feeling for the past as the re-awakener of old emotions. Rather, he delighted in fixing dreams and quickly perishing life in the form of brilliant arabesques. (This is more immediately recognized in the architecture of Andalusian mosques where floral nature is a continuous motif for an all-over surface design.) And if his fascination for the image itself did not overrule his sensibility entirely, he was interested ultimately in probing beyond the

22

landscape of the mutable, in lifting the trembling veil to come upon the one thing which stays permanently at rest.

Alongside the Arabic-Andalusian *casida* grew the tradition of the Spanish ballad, the *romance*. The *romance* developed as an accretion of many centuries out of the old epics (*cantares de gesta*), narrative poems celebrating the exploits of battle, the contributions of poetic schools like the Galician-Portuguese (*Cancioneros*) in the thirteenth and fourteenth centuries, and the work of individual poets like Juan de Mena, Juan del Encina, Gil Vicente, Luis de Góngora, Lope de Vega, and Calderón de la Barca who ushered in Spain's Golden Age. By repeating and reworking this balladry, the popular imagination preserved an historical testament of the life of the people. As a living tradition in all corners of the earth where Spanish is spoken, a prodigious collection of over fifty thousand ballad versions has been uncovered. This tradition explains why Spanish poetry finds a ready and spontaneous form, as it does immediate expression, without the burdensome manufacture of individual inventive systems so common to the literatures of other countries where poetry became detached much earlier from the people. At the same time, the popular tradition of the ballad afforded a "double" standard, a system of communicating experience on two levels—to the people and to the intellectual elite—which characterizes the work of every major Spanish poet, including Lorca.

They are often ballads of incident, faithfully describing a single historic event, as the frontier ballad about the capture of the city Álora from the Moors. What is emphasized is not the valor of grand gore-spilling heroes on the

FEDERICO GARCÍA LORCA

battlefield, but the realistic flight of the Moors and their
families to the top of the castle, and the wily strategy of a
Moorish defender who kills the invading chief, governor
of the province.

*Alora, la bien cercada,*
*tú que estás en par del río,*
*cercóte el Adelantado*
*una mañana de domingo,*
*de peones y hombres de armas*
*el campo bien guarnecido;*
*con la gran artillería*
*hecho te habían un portillo.*
*Viérades moros y moras*
*subir huyendo al castillo;*
*las moras llevan la ropa,*
*los moros harina y trigo,*
*y las moras de quince años*
*llevaban el oro fino,*
*y los moricos pequeños*
*llevan la pasa y el higo.*
*Por encima del adarve*
*su pendón llevan tendido.*
*Allá detrás de una almena*
*quedado se había un morico*
*con una ballesta armada*
*y en ella puesto un cuadrillo.*
*En altas voces diciendo*
*que del real le han oído;*
*—¡Tregua, tregua, adelantado,*
*por tuyo se da el castillo!*
*Alza la visera arriba*
*por ver el que tal le dijo:*
*asestárale a la frente,*
*salido le ha al colodrillo.*
*Sacólo Pablo de rienda*

24

# HIS HERITAGE

*y de mano Jacobillo,*
*estos dos que había criado*
*en su casa desde chicos.*
*Lleváronle a los maestros*
*por ver si será guarido;*
*a las primeras palabras*
*el testamento les dijo.*


(Álora, the strong walled,
you who lie along the river bank,
the Governor surrounded you
one morning on a Sunday,
the meadow fully flanked
with men at arms and peasantry.
They had forced a hole in you
with their heavy artillery.
See the Moorish men and women
fleeing up into the castle;
Moorish women bringing clothing,
Moorish men the flour and grain,
and Moorish girls of fifteen
bringing fine gold things,
while the tiny Moorish children
bring away the figs and raisins.
Atop the castle wall,
they hold their flag outstretched.
There behind a battlement,
a little Moor stood apart
with a cross-bow bent,
and in it a Moorish dart.
Shouting with so loud a roar
that they have heard him in the camp:
—Truce, truce, Governor,
the castle is given, it is yours!
He lifts his vizor overhead
to see the one who spoke:
shot straight to his forehead,

**25**

it left at the back of his neck.
Paul took the reins from him,
little Jacob took his hand,
those two who had been
raised from childhood on his land.
They carried him to their masters
to see if he could be saved;
but with his first words,
it was his testament he gave.)

Or they dwell with curious though typical insistence on
the triumph of death over love, as in the fifteenth century
ballad "El Enamorado y la Muerte" ("The Lover and
Death") [1]:

Un sueño soñaba anoche,
soñito del alma mía,
soñaba con mis amores
que en mis brazos los tenía.
Vi entrar señora tan blanca,
muy más que la nieve fría.
—¿Por dónde has entrado, amor?
¿Cómo has entrado, mi vida?
las puertas están cerradas,
ventanas y celosías.
—No soy el amor, amante:
la Muerte que Dios te envía.
—¡Ay, Muerte tan rigurosa,
déjame vivir un día!
—Un día no puede ser,
una hora tienes de vida.
Muy deprisa se calzaba,

[1] The shift from first to third person in this ballad is characteristic
of many of them, as is the rapid change from present to imperfect
or past tense.

26

*más de prisa se vestía;*
*ya se va para la calle,*
*en donde su amor vivía.*
*—¡Ábreme la puerta, blanca,*
*ábreme la puerta, niña!*
*—¿Cómo te podré yo abrir*
*si la ocasión no es venida?*
*Mi padre no fué al palacio,*
*mi madre no está dormida.*
*—Si no me abres esta noche,*
*ya no me abrirás, querida;*
*la Muerte me está buscando,*
*junto a ti vida sería.*
*—Vete bajo la ventana*
*donde labraba y cosía,*
*te echaré cordón de seda*
*para que subas arriba,*
*y si el cordón no alcanzare*
*mis trenzas añadiría.*
*La fina seda se rompe;*
*la Muerte que allí venía:*
*—Vamos, el enamorado,*
*que la hora ya está cumplida.*


(Last night I had a dream,
dear dream of my heart,
I dreamed I held all
my loved ones in my arms.
I saw a lady white come in,
much whiter than cold snow.
—Where do you come from, love?
How have you entered, my life?
The doors are all shut tight,
the windows and the lattices.
—I am not love, lover,
but Death God has sent you tonight.
—O Death, so stern and absolute,

**27**

let me live another day!
—A day it cannot be,
you've an hour more to stay.
He quickly clothed his feet,
more quickly did he dress;
and now running down the street
to where his loved one stayed.
—Open the door for me, love,
open the door, my maid!
—How can I let you in,
if the time has not yet come?
My father not in the palace,
my mother not yet asleep.
—If you don't open the door tonight,
my love, you'll never open it.
Death is looking for me,
but near you Life must be.
—Stand under the window
where I embroider and sew,
I'll throw you a silk cord
to climb up this way,
and if the cord is short,
I'll add my own braids.
The fine silk is broken;
Death had then come in:
—Lover, let us go,
for your hour is now over.)

Or they are ballads which dramatize the mystic call of
the unknown, as the one in which the young prince Arnaldos happens to hear the sea song of an unknown sailor:

¡Quién hubiera tal ventura
sobre las aguas del mar
como hubo el infante Arnaldos
la mañana de San Juan!

# HIS HERITAGE

*Andando a buscar la caza*
*para su falcón cebar,*
*vió venir una galera*
*que a tierra quiere llegar;*
*las velas trae de sedas,*
*la ejarcia de oro torzal,*
*áncoras tiene de plata,*
*tablas de fino coral.*
*Marinero que la guía,*
*diciendo viene un cantar,*
*que la mar ponía en calma,*
*los vientos hace amainar;*
*los peces que andan al hondo,*
*arriba los hace andar;*
*las aves que van volando,*
*al mástil vienen posar.*
*Allí habló el infante Arnaldos,*
*bien oréis lo que dirá:*
*—Por tu vida, el marinero,*
*dígasme ora ese cantar.*
*Respondióle el marinero,*
*tal respuesta le fué a dar:*
*—Yo no digo mi canción*
*sino a quien conmigo va.*

(Who would have had such fortune
by the waters of the sea
as the royal prince Arnaldos
on the morning of St. John!
Out hunting for game
for his falcon to feed on,
he saw a galley come
edging up to the land;
the sails she bears are silken,
her mast of twisted gold,
her anchors made of silver
and planks of perfect coral.

The sailor who manned her
comes in with a song
which made the sea grow calm
and all the winds die down,
made fishes on the bottom
swim up to the top;
the birds who go by flying
turn on the mast to stop.
Then the royal prince spoke,
hear well what he'll say:
—O sailor, on your life,
teach me that song, I pray.
The sailor made his reply,
and such an answer gave:
—I do not teach my song save
to him who comes with me.)

Contained within this ballad tradition is an unusually rich amalgam of racial experience, an expression of the people's peculiar genius to retrieve the best elements from Spain's many cultural inundations. The tendency to assimilate whatever touches the country's essential spirit makes Spanish literature a highly adaptable organism invigorated by each successive wave. In this process, the stature of her great writers is dwarfed, so that the best frequently seem hardly a head above the most indifferent. Spanish literature is never "represented" by one or two writers, but by all, or most of them, at once. It is constantly hovering over the margin where the individual expression passes into the anonymous, where what seems the most anonymous is actually the work of the most individual of artists. It is a literature that is forever contracting and expanding like the heart, with the action of a constant, self-replenishing bloodstream. During periods of foreign invasion and subjection, it contracts to within a shadow of itself, only to burst forth again, inspirited to new proportions. It is essentially mystic in that it grows by rediscovering itself; yet it is also realistic in that it never relinquishes what is once claimed as its own.

An important specific aspect of this literature was the poetic baroque, a stylistic synthesis of materials created in the poetry of Luis de Góngora. Only recently has the merit of this seventeenth century contribution been seriously appraised. The efforts of modern Spanish poets and critics to resurrect Góngora from obscurity have provided an important insight into the historical modes of poetic composition in Spain.[1] What kept Góngora in the discard for so long was the unchallenged opinion of scholars that since he wrote both traditional ballads, in the popular manner, and poems like *Polifemo* and *Soledades*, woven in a maze of syntactical and metaphorical intricacies, he must have harbored within himself an "angel of light" (the good one!) and an "angel of darkness" (the bad one!). The critic Dámaso Alonso has taken pains to disprove this by showing that both approaches were actually logical and coherent aspects of the one artistic personality. Rather than two mutually exclusive manners in Góngora's work, Alonso argues, there are two contemporary styles, two attitudes innate not only to Góngora but to the temperament of Spain itself, with its enthusiastic and its skeptic views towards life.

[1] There is a close resemblance between these efforts of poets and critics to excavate and to reinstate the Góngora esthetic in Spain and the efforts of critic-poets like Eliot to bring Donne and the seventeenth century "metaphysicals" back into the bloodstream of English poetry.

Throughout his career, Góngora wrote many charming *letrillas* ("rondelets") and satiric ballads at the same time that he wrote songs and sonnets with the more canny interest of uplifting poetry esthetically. This duality in feeling and method is characteristic of all Spanish literature during the Renaissance, Spain's Golden Age. From the *Celestina* to the *Quijote,* from Gil Vicente to Lope de Vega, there is in each work and author a double imaginative vision: one part turned toward the Middle Ages, the other toward the Renaissance—an expression of life on the plane of necessity and an expression of life on the plane of contingency. The difficulty of Góngora's language is a direct result of the hybrid poetic styles existing in Spain from the twelfth to the sixteenth centuries. Thus, far from revolutionizing Spanish poetry, Góngora stressed its deep traditional character by synthesizing all the uses of baroque and popular styles current since the Middle Ages. By such emphasis, he also created his own individual style. The work of Góngora's so-called period of darkness was simply an intensification of stylistic habits which developed from his work in the popular manner. The same process of intensification in Góngora's style suggests a larger material synthesis: the condensation of all elements of the Renaissance lyric, which in itself was a Spanish synthesis of the Greco-Latin tradition. This indicates that poetry as a cultural expression of the age in which it is written can amalgamate the traditions arising from a long racial experience. It is a noteworthy coincidence that Lorca shows the same tendency, in constructing what seems a purely autonomous world, to synthesize

32

the traditional techniques of Spanish expression continuing from the Middle Ages.[1]

An an Andalusian, Góngora shared the same wonder for the landscape of seductive nature that stimulated the Arabic poets. Like them, he was anxious to solidify the fleeting world in the poetic form of jewelled monuments. It is the single intent running through his simple ballads and the mosaic-work of *Soledades* (*Solitudes*). For always in the midst of a clear sparkling flow, we encounter an arrested movement, when the poet stops to work out the minute section of a design which interests him more than the rest:

> *El cristal de aquel arroyo,*
> *Undosamente fiel,*
> *Niega al ausente su imagen*
> *Hasta que lo vuelve a ver.*

> (The glass of that stream,
> undulantly loyal,
> denies the absent one his image
> till he return to see it.)

[1] William Blake in his *Prophetic Books* created a poetic world which at first sight seems as forbiddingly obscure as Góngora's. He was really posing a system of imaginative thought, through the use of Biblical and pagan symbolism, to be an effective counterweight to both the scientific hypothesis of "pure reason" and the false apologetics for religion in his age. More recently, Yeats, led by the nose into all kinds of spiritistic disciplines, sought to emulate Blake in the same way. A poetic synthesis of cultural ideas does not simply mirror the beliefs current in the contemporary world but selects, condenses and intensifies materials from human experience through the ages in the form of a personal imaginative synthesis which is at once modern and timeless.

33

And again, in describing the bonfires which after their glorious blaze slowly die out in the night, he says:

> Los fuegos—cuyas lenguas, ciento a ciento,
> desmintieron la noche algunas horas,
> cuyas luces, de el Sol competidoras,
> fingieron día en la tiniebla oscura—
> murieron, y en sí mismos sepultados,
> sus miembros en cenizas desatados
> piedras son de su misma sepultura.

> (The fires—whose hundredfold tongues
> contradicted the night a few hours,
> whose lights, rivals of the sun,
> feigned day in pitch darkness—
> fell dead, and, buried in themselves,
> their limbs unhinged in ashes
> are gravestones on their own tombs.)

Yet it is this same poet who can also use the popular ballad form with simple and direct artistry to depict a girl forsaken by her lover:

> Lloraba la niña
> (y tenía razon)
> la prolija ausencia
> de su ingrato amor.
> Dejóla tan niña,
> que apenas creo yo
> que tenía los años
> que ha que la dejó.
> Llorando la ausencia
> del galán traidor,
> la halla la Luna
> y la deja el Sol,
> añadiendo siempre
> pasión a pasión,

> memoria a memoria,
> dolor a dolor.

> Llorad, corazón,
> que tenéis razón.

> Dícele su madre:
> "Hija, por mi amor,
> que se acabe el llanto
> o me acabe yo."
> Ella le responde:
> "No podrá ser, no;
> las causas son muchas,
> los ojos son dos.

34

# HIS HERITAGE

Satisfagan, madre,
tanta sinrazón,
y lágrimas lloren,
en esta ocasión,
tantas como dellos
un tiempo tiró
flechas amorosas
el arquero Dios.
Ya no canto, madre,
y si canto yo,

muy tristes endechas
mis canciones son;
porque el que se fué,
con lo que llevó,
se dejó el silencio
y llevó la voz."

Llorad, corazón,
que tenéis razón.

(The young girl mourned
—and she had reason—
the absence prolonged
of her ungrateful love.
He left her so young
that I scarcely believe
her years were so many then
as those since he left her.
Mourning the absence
of her gallant deceiver,
she is found by the Moon
and is left by the Sun,
adding forever
passion to passion,
memory to memory,
sorrow to sorrow.

Weep, my heart, for you
have reason to.

Says her mother to her,
"Child, by my love,
end your lament

or my end will come."
The girl answers her,
"It cannot be, no,
the causes are many,
my eyes only two;
let such unreason,
mother, satisfy you.
And for this occasion,
let as many tears drop
as those arrows of love
which the archer god
Cupid once shot.
Mother, I cannot sing now,
and if I do sing,
my songs are dirges
heavy with sorrow,
for the one who is gone,
with what he took away,
has left me the silence
and stolen my voice."

Weep, my heart, for you
have reason to.)

Góngora exalts reality till, caught in its flight, it is suddenly converted into a version of permanence. It is a

35

world which differs from the poetic construction of the
Symbolists in that every object is represented in its own
sufficiency and dignity, the perfection of its very nature,
and does not swarm about in the nether-world seeking
the idea for which it must substitute. Also distinct from
modern surrealism, it is a world of formal architectural
pattern, an organization of tamed nature, and not the
imposition of confusion on a half-perceived nature, an
unassimilated reality. Not until Lorca was Spanish poetry
again able to treat the phenomenal world with as much
plastic sensitivity and technical mastery as Góngora.

Another cultural facet of the Spanish literary tradition
is the contribution of outcast gypsy tribes. Lorca himself,
gifted with a fine musical sense, was, with Manuel de
Falla, one of the principal exponents of Andalusian gypsy
music in modern Spain. Gypsy tribes of undetermined
origin entered Spain in the fifteenth century and brought
to the Byzantine and Arabic elements of Andalusian song
a new tonal character. This combination goes by the name
of *cante jondo*, "deep song." Bearing close analogy to the
hieratic melodies of India and the primitive Christian
chant, *cante jondo* is a curious, almost orgiastic lament, a
composite expression of the sacred and pagan experience
of many ancient peoples. Musically it is based on the
obsessive repetition of certain phrases, or even of single
notes, to the point where the whole meter of the verse to
which it is being sung appears lost—as in certain aspects
of enchantment, the pitch of the voice so curdles the blood
that the meaning of the words has gone out of the ritual.
At one time, Andalusia was filled with professional troubadours (*cantaores*), who travelled from village to village,

improvising the music of *cante jondo* to popular ballads, or to original verses of their own. During the last few decades, the institution of the *cantaor* rapidly reached extinction, and with it the original "deep song." A few surviving *cantaores* remained: Juan Breva, who was attached to the court of Alfonso XIII, and José Cepero, who was once heard singing to the verses of Rafael Alberti, the contemporary poet, in a Sevillian tavern.

Most of the improvisations of the *cantaores* have not been collected, and are still known mainly through oral tradition. The characteristic form of invention is the *copla*. Like the *romance,* the verses are usually divided into eight-syllable lines, and in content may be narrative, lyrical, political, religious, or anything, in fact, which will entertain and be easy to repeat. A short example of a *copla* by José Cepero may suggest the animated spirit in which it is composed:

> *A un arroyo claro a beber,*
> *a un arroyo claro a beber,*
> *vi bajar una paloma.*
>
> *Por no mojarse la cola,*
> *levantó el vuelo y se fué.*
> *¡Qué paloma tan señora!*

> (While drinking at a clear little brook,
> While drinking at a clear little brook,
> I saw a dove alight.
>
> So as not to get her tail wet,
> she raised her wing and fled.
> A dove so lady-like!)

At the time of the Napoleonic invasion of Spain when Goya was mordantly commemorating *Los Desastres de la Guerra* (*The Disasters of the War*), many *coplas* went the rounds satirizing the invaders. This is one of them:

> Con el plomo que tiran
> los fanfarrones,
> se hacen las gaditanas
> tirabuzones.
>
> Con las balas que tira
> el Mariscal Suhl,
> se hacen las gaditanas
> mantillas de tul.
>
> (Out of the lead shot by
> the bullying liars,
> the ladies of Cádiz make
> curling irons.
>
> Out of the bullets shot by
> Marshal Suhl,
> the ladies of Cádiz make
> mantillas of tulle.)

During Holy Week in Spain, the processions in the streets re-enacting the Passion of Christ are accompanied by an eery music of trumpet and drum to which verses called *saetas* (literally, "darts" of song) are sung. Here are two such *saetas*:

> Con ese cuerpo llagado,
> lleno de sangre y afrenta,
> pareces clavel morado
> lleno de perlas sangrientes.

# HIS HERITAGE

*Por allí viene San Juan*
*vestido de rojo y verde,*
*llorando detrás de Cristo*
*las culpas que tú cometes.*

(With a body so tortured,
full of blood and outrage,
you seem a purple carnation
full of bloody pearls.

And there comes St. John,
in red and green bedecked,
lamenting behind Jesus
the sins which you commit.)

Before the recent Spanish war, a revival of *cante jondo*
brought new singing blood to the ballad tradition, and
troubadours wandering through the country often sang
to modern verses as their forbears had sung to popular
ballads in the fifteenth and sixteenth centuries. The gypsy
lament, heavy with the atmosphere of blood and death,
and flooded with the tragic feeling of an outcast people,
is the supreme expression of anonymity in Andalusian
music and poetry. Its rich rhythmic flexibility and extended vocal inflections transmuted into Lorca's verse produced fascinating discords seldom heard before in European poetry.

Even before Lorca had begun to write his first poems,
an impressive poetic renaissance had already occurred in
Spain. The principal figures contributing to this movement were Rubén Darío, Miguel de Unamuno, Antonio
and Manuel Machado, and Juan Ramón Jiménez. While
their work re-inforced the traditional ballad, it also intro-

duced new forms derived from French, German and English poetry. In the synthetic manner of Góngora, Rubén Darío, the Nicaraguan who was the greatest poet writing in Spanish before Lorca, re-discovered the medieval *cantares,* the old Latin-Spanish hexameters, and every stray metrical form of the Golden Age poets. He purified the Castilian language by raising it from the imitative sloughs of French neo-classicism and Parnassianism. Technically, Darío's contribution is perhaps unparalleled in the history of Spanish poetry. His rich adaptive techniques proved Spanish versification as flexible and various as any in European literature. Moreover, he revealed a temperamental affinity between the musical line of Verlaine and the French Symbolists and Spain's own antique ballad tradition. Yet he was unable to lift his art out of the typical *fin-de-siècle malaise.* It became an exaggerated show of decadence to which Spanish poetry was ill-suited; and Darío died with Mallarmé's tragic alcoholic fawn nibbling at his heart.

Almost contemporaneous with Darío came the robust mystical ardor of Unamuno's poetry. Though lacking Darío's technical genius, Unamuno was compensated by a profound spiritual maturity. Unamuno touched the heart of Spain's religious passion at the same point where Luis de León, Santa Teresa, and San Juan de la Cruz had made it bleed. Like them, he displayed the same terrifying energy in pursuit of practical missions with which he felt his initial preoccupation—a creative religious faith—to be bound. Unamuno's verses are the free expressions of a quixotic spirit, multitudinously contradictory and heretical, seeking the form of the litany and working with the same dual consciousness of the popular and sophisticated forms as the Golden Age poets. If Darío was the revolutionary from without, the master of brilliant metaphor, the prestidigitator with metrical forms, Unamuno—who could also write the solidest Spanish prose of his age—was the revolutionary from within, master of the spirit, with a quick, burly sense of the fatally unresolved metaphysics implicit in any system of human faith.

Lorca's most immediate influences were the Andalusians Antonio and Manuel Machado, and Juan Ramón Jiménez. Continuing the traditional exaltation of the diminutive, the anecdotal, and the ironic style of Andalusian genius, Antonio Machado's poetry is free from the complicated social and esthetic heresies of modern art. He glorifies the elemental forms of the natural world; without didacticism, and without adhering to a poetic school, he infuses an antique landscape with a powerful personal mysticism. Yet his accent, as shown in such a poem as "Rosa de Fuego" ("Rose of Fire"), is essentially modern and universal:

> *Tejidos sois de primavera, amantes,*
> *de tierra y agua y viento y sol tejidos.*
> *La sierra en vuestros pechos jadeantes,*
> *en los ojos los campos florecidos,*
>
> *pasead vuestra mutua primavera,*
> *y aun bebed sin temor la dulce leche*
> *que os brinda hoy la lúbrica pantera,*
> *antes que, torva, en el camino aceche.*

*Caminad, cuando el eje del planeta*
*se vence hacia el solsticio de verano,*
*verde el almendro y mustia la violeta,*

*cerca la sed y el hontanar cercano,*
*hacia la tarde del amor, completa,*
*con la rosa de fuego en vuestra mano.*

(You are woven of Spring, lovers,
woven of earth and water, sun and wind.
The plain in your throbbing breasts,
in your eyes the flowering fields,

walk with your mutual Spring,
and drink still without fear the sweet milk
the slippery panther offers you today,
before fiercely, in the road, he lies in wait.

Stroll when the earth's axis
leans on the summer solstice,
the almond tree green, and languid the violet,

near drought and the nearby fountains,
toward the afternoon of love, complete,
with the rose of fire in your hand.)

Although the work of Manuel Machado was not impressed so deeply upon his contemporaries, nor was it ever as insistently searching as that of his brother Antonio or of Jiménez, it is important as an early literary adaptation of the Andalusian folk song. When he is not posturing in the manner of French romantic insouciance, Manuel Machado is genuinely Spanish in the traditional spirit of the ballad, as in the poem "Lirio" ("Lily"), where he fits Gerineldos, the daring lover of an old ballad, into the modern scene:

# HIS HERITAGE

*Casi todo alma,*
*vaga Gerineldos*
*por esos jardines*
*del rey, a lo lejos,*
*junto a los macizos*
*de arrayanes . . . Besos*
*de la reina dicen*
*los morados circos*
*de sus ojos mustios,*
*dos idilos muertos.*
*Casi todo alma,*

*se pierde en silencio*
*por el laberinto*
*de arrayanes . . . ¡Besos!*
*solo, solo, solo.*
*Lejos, lejos, lejos . . .*
*Como una humareda,*
*como un pensamiento . . .*
*como esa persona*
*extraña, que vemos*
*cruzar por las calles*
*oscuras de un sueño.*

(Almost all soul,
Gerineldos wanders
through the gardens
of the king, far away,
near the walls
of myrtles . . . Kisses
from the queen, say
the purple rings
about his languid eyes,
two dead idyls.
Almost all soul,

he is lost in silence
through the labyrinth
of myrtles . . . Kisses!
Alone, alone, alone.
Far-away, away, away . . .
like a cloud of smoke,
like a thought . . .
like that strange
person we see
crossing the dark
streets of a dream.)

And in a sudden short poem like "Madrigal," he touches lightly a typical aspect of Spanish fatalism:

*Y no será una noche*
*sublime de huracán, en que las olas*
*toquen los cielos . . . Tu barquillo leve*
*naufragará de día, un día claro*
*en que el mar esté alegre.*
*Te matarán jugando. Es el destino*
*terrible de los débiles . . .*
*Mientras un sol espléndido*
*sube al cenit, hermoso como siempre.*

(And it will not be a sublime
night of hurricanes, in which waves
touch the skies . . . Your flimsy little
boat will be wrecked by day, a bright
day in which the sea is gay.
They will kill you while you play.
It is the terrible destiny of the weak . . .
While a splendid sun rises
to its heights, handsome as always.)

Jiménez harmonized the refined musical tones of the
Andalusian lament with the visual elements of a deep
color impressionism. A short epigrammatic poem like
"Canción" gives the composite effect of music and color:

> Todo el otoño, rosa,
> es esa sola hoja tuya
> que cae.

> Niña, todo el dolor
> es esa sola gota tuya
> de sangre.

> (Rose, the whole of autumn
> lies in your single petal
> falling.

> Little girl, the whole of sorrow
> lies in a single drop of your
> blood.)

Jiménez went to school with the German Romantics, the
French Symbolists, and the Irish Nationalist poets, and
thus created a valuable esthetic instrument for his art. The
Andalusia of garden and sea is the subject of most of his

44

short lyric poems. In these he perfected the miniature forms of the landscape with a water colorist's imagination. He pursues a mystical estheticism by which his inner landscape may grow rich from the substance it gathers and refines of the never ending luxuriance of the country. An early poem, "Nocturno" ("Nocturne"), indicates this life-long occupation of his:

> *La luna me echa en el alma*
> *honda, un agua de deslumbres,*
> *que me la deja lo mismo*
> *que un pozo templado y dulce.*
>
> *Entonces, mi fondo, bueno*
> *para todos, sube, sube,*
> *y abre, al nivel del prado*
> *del mundo, su agua de luces.*
>
> *Agua que une estrella y flor,*
> *que llama a la sed con lumbres*
> *celestes, donde están, náufragos*
> *de amor, los reinos azules.*
>
> (The moon throws deep into
> my soul a water of dazzling
> lights, which leaves it
> like a well, warm and sweet.
>
> Then my depths, good
> for everyone, rise, rise up
> and open to the level of the world's
> meadow its water of lights.
>
> Water uniting star and flower,
> calling to thirst with celestial
> lights, where, like those shipwrecked
> by love, lie the blue kingdoms.)

45

The poetry of Jiménez exists in the sheer flow of an incessant crystalline stream, absorbing the simplest forms of light variation—a preservation of small unsleeping life in the death-ridden heart of Andalusia.

This, then, is the heritage of materials from which Lorca began to write. And learning the responsibility of form, he continued to rely on these domains of the Spanish tradition as freely and necessarily as a lord on vassals whose worth is proven, and in whose trust he sees himself forever tested.

## 3. THE EMBATTLED GARDEN—EARLY VERSE

LORCA'S WORK FALLS QUITE EASILY INTO TWO PERIODS. THE first, from 1918 to 1930, includes the major portion of his poetic composition and only an experimental beginning in the dramatic. In the second period, after the summer of 1930 and until his death in 1936, Lorca's efforts turned mainly to the drama; that is, with the exception of the major poem, *Llanto por Ignacio Sánchez Mejías,* and the unedited volume of verse, *El Diván del Tamarit.* While convenient for purposes of discussion, such a neat division inappropriately suggests two mutually exclusive occupations, one in poetry and the other in drama. Actually, his poetic and his dramatic works are two sides of a single coin which cannot be allowed to rest for a moment on either side. To enlarge the metaphor: the coin spinning on its edge is kept in motion by the subtle interplay between two dimensions—the poetic and the dramatic—in the artistic personality. Thus, there is nothing in Lorca's poetry which does not suggest dramatic projection; and, likewise, in Lorca's drama there is no situation or theme which does not emerge through the poetic imagination. Here the ordinary insistence on the distinction between the two media ceases to be an essential problem. The major concern of the following chapters will be to examine Lorca's art as a product of this interaction.

To the degree that a poet's growth is a refinement of his initial preoccupations, his earliest work becomes a definitive signature of sensibility—his unique apprehension of the natural world, projected into a convincing poetic relationship. In poets of considerable singleness of purpose, like Lorca, it is often easier to make out this signature from the start than at further points in their development where more complicated techniques and the implications of wider experience impinge upon the original clarity of outline. Thus, Lorca's first poems, though following in the steps of the spiritually underfed Symbolists, are yet distinctive for their re-creation of landscape as a state of the soul, an outer version of the inner world— the effort of projection which motivates all his work. His *Libro de Poemas* (1921) is the poetry of insomnia, of nights and days turning like huge pages of the memory which he scans to capture light and darkness, the heart of generation and decay, in order to convert them into song. He does not want a world in shadow, for he is above all a realistic sensualist who must have the secret of light bare. But if the moment goes with all its glory only to be replaced by one still more glorious, then memory itself is a falsification of the senses, giving the lie to the reflected image and the momentary exaltation. Hence he must seek an objective form to express the never-ending moment. This he finds, for instance, in the pomegranate:

> *Mas la granada es la sangre,*
> *Sangre del cielo sagrado,*
> *Sangre de la tierra herida*
> *Por la aguja del regato.*
> *Sangre del viento que viene*
> *Del rudo monte arañado.*
> *Sangre de la mar tranquila,*
> *Sangre del dormido lago.*
> *La granada es la prehistoria*
> *De la sangre que llevamos,*
> *La idea de sangre, encerrada*
> *En glóbulo duro y agrio,*
> *Que tiene una vaga forma*
> *De corazón y de cráneo.*

> (But the pomegranate is the blood,
> Blood of blessed heaven,
> Blood of earth wounded
> By the needle of a stream.
> Blood of the wind that comes
> Scraping off rough mountains.
> Blood of the quiet sea,
> Blood of the sleeping lake.
> The pomegranate is the burden
> Of prehistory in our blood,
> The idea of blood enclosed
> In the hard and bitter globule,
> That has a vague form
> Of heart and skull.)

With the thirst of his ancient predecessors, the medieval Arabic-Andalusian poets, Lorca attempts to raid the eternal immutable that rests somewhere beyond the veil of the senses. But like them, he is too involved in the flux to lose himself in an abstract spiritual quest. He seeks, instead, a peculiarly metamorphic nature where light wants to be sound, and sound wants to be air, where a river wants to be a stone. His world is a microscopic garden magnified until it seems almost a forest. Yet, sighing or raging, it yields no more tragedy than the sensual pain of botanical warfare going on in the poet's own consciousness. He says, "Tuve la gran tristeza vegetal. . . ." ("I had the great vegetable sadness. . . ."). When grief in his garden becomes exhausted, he continues to weave out ever more stylized arabesques, till finally the garden takes on the tamed appearance of a Gongoristic landscape:

> *Se ha puesto el sol. Los árboles*
> *Meditan como estatuas.*
>
> .     .     .     .     .
>
> *Los mosquitos—Pegasos del rocío—*
> *Vuelan al aire en calma.*
> *La Penélope inmensa de la luz*
> *Teje una noche clara.*
>
> (The sun has set. Trees
> Ruminate like statues.
>
> .     .     .     .     .
>
> Mosquitoes, Pegasi of dew,
> Hover through quiet air.
> The immense Penelope of light
> Weaves out a brilliant night.)

It is always this sharp Latin spirit, the inventive intellect which displaces a fervid, overworked imagination. On the other hand, Lorca's musical propensities are intensified in compensation. For at the same time he is directed to the simple stream of song:

### Los Niños

*¿Quién te enseñó el camino*
*De los poetas?*

### Yo

*La fuente y el arroyo*
*De la canción añeja.*

### Los Niños

*¿Te vas lejos, muy lejos*
*Del mar y de la tierra?*

### Yo

*Se ha llenado de luces*
*Mi corazón de seda,*
*De campanas perdidas,*
*De lirios y de abejas,*
*Y yo me iré muy lejos,*
*Más allá de esas sierras,*
*Más allá de los mares*
*Cerca de las estrellas,*
*Para pedirle a Cristo*
*Señor que me devuelva*
*Mi alma antigua de niño,*
*Madura de leyendas,*
*Con el gorro de plumas*
*Y el sable de madera.*

### (Children

Who showed you
The poet's way?

51

*I*

The fountain and brook
Of antique song.

*Children*

Are you going far, very far
From land and sea?

*I*

My heart of silk
Is filled with lights
Of lost bells,
Of lilies and bees,
And I'll travel very far,
Farther than those hills,
Farther than the seas,
Close to the stars,
To ask my Lord Jesus
To return my old
Child's heart,
Saturated with legends,
With the plumed cap,
And the wooden sabre.)

Buffeted between themes of romantic nostalgia and self
conscious adolescent despair, Lorca often finds in the
haven of childhood that innocence which purifies and
directs the heart. When in the same poem, "Balada de la
Placeta" ("Ballad of the Little Square"), the poet is asked
by the children what he feels in his mouth "thirsty and
red," and he replies, "the savor of the bones of my large
skull," we come upon the first evidence of the preoccupation with death which is to fill his whole work. And com-
plementing this preoccupation, briefly suggested in *Libro
de Poemas,* is an emergent sense of conflict between

dreaming innocence and a ready-made stubborn reality, which hints at the major theme of his later dramatic writing.

*Libro de Poemas* is contained within a landscape that is partly the poet's own invention, partly that of other poets, like Juan Ramón Jiménez. Here the untried spirit sobs, innocent and hungry, and quickly molded by the trickery of appearances in an all too *visible* world. No biological catastrophe enters to spill blood on the unworried flowers. Death is a little woman, Doña Muerte, the sometime paramour of God, Himself a merciless little Jehovah whom the poet both scoffs at and dreads with child-like credulity. All creation is a metaphor in the poet's mind, a diminutive effigy in the dream of a child, the riotous mosaic vision of the cicada who dies "drunk with light." But that other light of consciousness, human responsibility, is unawakened.

In Lorca's next book,[1] the imaginative flow is started in another direction. *Poema del Cante Jondo* (*Poem of Deep Song*) constitutes a complete lyrical acceptance of the popular spirit. The symbols of the typical Andalusian gypsy song are condensed and restyled. The rivers of Granada are caught like "little bulls dead in the pools"; "the olive field opens and closes like a fan;" and the lament of the guitar "breaks the goblets of dawn." Everywhere the poet sees "the dagger in the heart"; "everything in the world has been broken"; "nothing remains but si-

---

[1] *Poema del Cante Jondo* was completed in 1921, though it was not published as a volume until 1931. Through numerous revisions, the poet had given the individual poems by that time a perfection of which he was obviously incapable earlier.

lence." The only reality is the dance and the six chords of the guitar from whose "overflowing mouth" the "sobs of lost souls escape." The gypsy world provides Lorca with those motives informing all primitive song: a twilight half-joy half-fear, and the full night of death. Here for the first time he is confronted by the anonymity of death as the bolder and larger counterpart to the painful unrest of his gardens:

> Muerto se quedó en la calle
> con un puñal en el pecho.
> No lo conocía nadie.
> ¡Cómo temblaba el farol!
> Madre.
> ¡Cómo temblaba el farolito
> de la calle!
> Era madrugada. Nadie
> pudo asomarse a sus ojos
> abiertos al duro aire.
> Que muerto se quedó en la calle
> que con un puñal en el pecho
> y que no lo conocía nadie.

> (Left dead in the street,
> a dagger in his breast,
> he was recognized by no one.
> Mother, how the street-light
> trembled!
> How the little lantern
> trembled!
> It was dawn. Nobody
> could peep into his eyes,
> opened on solid air.
> For, left dead in the street,
> a dagger in his heart,
> he was recognized by no one.)

54

And he finds the ancient Andalusian cities haunted by the same weight of deathly inquietude that hungers for expressive form in his own songs:

> *Y loca de horizonte*
> *mezcla en su vino*
> *lo amargo de Don Juan*
> *y lo perfecto de Dionisio.*

> (And mad with horizon
> it mixes in its wine
> the bitterness of Don Juan
> and the perfection of Dionysus.)

More minutely exploring the cultural evidences of the region, he identifies in his poems the emotional connotations found in "El Paso de la Siguiriya," "La Soleá," "La Saeta," "La Petenera," and "Malagüeña." They are small vignettes of Andalusian life opening on a landscape where everything dissolves in a cry, in the movement of a hundred horsemen, in the trembling notes of the guitar, and in the familiar entrance of death, who, if not disguised as a woman, becomes the abrupt monotony of a tavern door swinging back and forth:

> *La muerte*
> *entra y sale*
> *de la taberna.*

> *Pasan caballos negros*
> *y gente siniestra*
> *por los hondos caminos*
> *de la guitarra.*

**55**

*Y hay un olor a sal*
*y a sangre de hembra*
*en los nardos febriles*
*de la marina.*

*La muerte*
*entra y sale,*
*y sale y entra*
*la muerte*
*de la taberna.*

( Death
comes and goes
through the tavern.

Black horses
and sinister men
pass through the deep roads
of the guitar.

There's a smell of salt
and woman's blood
in the warm tuberoses
of the sea.

Death
comes and goes,
and death
goes and comes
through the tavern.)

Something of his adolescent grief has been washed out
in *Poema del Cante Jondo*. The poet has found through
statement and re-statement, and through apparently art-
less but effective accumulation, a form which is dramatically powerful and artistically unassailable as a representation of folk feeling. In the manner of the original *cante*

*jondo,* Lorca has transmuted the musical characteristics of the broken voice into the repetition of a single refrain. It is true that the presentation of Death in these terms is still stylized. But if used as an artifice here, death itself grows more and more basic to the poet's conceptions. Lorca's poems, inspired by the ancient tradition of *cante jondo,* are in their way only echoes and re-echoes of a cultural experience more profound than one man's vision can hope to encompass. Yet precisely at such a point—where the poet discovers and utilizes a tradition—he encounters himself, as it were, for the first time. The deeper consciousness he achieves in communion with that tradition will determine his later development. For, through the processes of imaginative re-creation, he learns to differentiate what is false to his poetry from what is essential. He is given new incentive to seek the forms in which his particular burden will find the articulation it deserves. From the gypsies, Lorca gradually learned that the fixities, the constants of natural law, were the lessons which had somehow escaped the modern world. What was given him as practically a gift at birth—the capacity for, the quick discernment of, human suffering—were precisely those sympathies which were quickly atrophying in societies more heterogeneous than that of Andalusia. But the full tragedy of such stunting of the modern conscience was only to penetrate his poetry later, when for a short time he left the translucent world of Granada to come to New York, "the Senegal of steel." With *Poema del Cante Jondo,* Lorca realized the new folk power of his poetic material. Essentially he had begun to focus his vision on this single element. In both form and direction his later work becomes

**57**

an enlargement and elaboration of his original folk interest: the ballad, the mystic-lyrical revelations of instinct, and the attempt to create a permanent esthetic in which this material may be universalized.

His book *Canciones*, though still echoing the cries of a restless botanical world, indicates a new turn in his lyricism. Esthetically, his interest has shifted from the loose anthropomorphism of *Libro de Poemas* to a plastic concern with natural objects, at the same time that his earlier rhythms have widened into a personal adaptation of the gypsy song. Here, Lorca invents contrapuntal melodies wherein the opposition of a dual theme is constantly seeking resolution in a single harmony, somewhat in the manner of the simple fugue. Lorca also uses abrupt shifts in image and rhythm which produce the startling effects peculiar to Spanish music, when key is repeatedly changed and time is suddenly broken and quickened or slowed:

> *Mi manzano*
> *tiene ya sombra y pájaros.*
>
> *¡Qué brinco da mi sueño*
> *de la luna al viento!*
>
> *Mi manzano*
> *da a lo verde sus brazos.*
>
> *Desde Marzo, ¡como veo*
> *la frente blanca de Enero!*
>
> *Mi manzano . . .*
> *(viento bajo).*
>
> *Mi manzano . . .*
> *(cielo alto).*

(My apple tree
now has birds and shade.

What a leap my dream makes
from the moon into the wind!

My apple tree
gives its arms to greenness.

From March, how clearly I see
the white forehead of January!

My apple tree . . .
(wind below).

My apple tree . . .
(sky above).

Or his words, like hammer and chisel, sculpture scenes more durable than the fierce moment in which they were given him to see. He has eliminated the nostalgic discursiveness of *Libro de Poemas* with its unresolved and diffuse pantheism. Instead, his images are objectified and made abrasive because he concentrates on the plastic qualities of objects. In this way, he succeeds in delineating a sumptuous nature by an economy of specific references. This is illustrated in the simple construction of the poem "Agosto" ("August"):

Agosto,
contraponientes
de melocotón y azúcar,
y el sol dentro de la tarde,
como el hueso de una fruta.
La panocha guarda intacta,
su risa amarilla y dura.
Agosto.

**59**

*Los niños comen*
*pan moreno y rica luna.*

> (August,
> counterpoints
> of sugar and peach,
> and the sun within the afternoon
> like a fruit's core.
>     The ear of grain keeps intact
> its hard yellow laughter.
>     August.
> Children eat
> brown bread and delicious moon.)

Lorca's language here is as instinctive as his vision; or, better, it impresses one as the immediate instinct of vision. It is in some sense true of the weakness and strength of all his poetry that the direct perception of reality, his fabulous treasury of feeling, is constantly escaping the esthetic mold into which his intellect attempts to cast it. The *Canciones* indicates a vigorous effort to dominate the fluidity of his imagination with artistic form. Each poem seems to gasp under the weight of the intent, and wrenching itself free, to escape as soon as the last word has been written. What is true of the formal design is no less true of the thematic. There is already the consciousness that just as he must organize his form, he must also regiment his menagerie of botanical and zoological life into a mythology—a mythology in which the only human intruders are children. Yet always, the discipline is somehow eluded and his mythology never properly enters the world of legend since his creatures are only too adept at accomplishing their own metamorphosis:

*Los días de fiesta*
*van sobre ruedas.*
*El tíovivo los trae*
*y los lleva.*
   *Corpus azul.*
*Blanca nochebuena.*

.   .   .   .

   *El tíovivo gira*
*colgado de una estrella.*
*Tulipán de las cinco*
*partes de la tierra.*
   *Sobre caballitos*
*disfrazados de panteras*
*los niños se comen la luna*
*como si fuera una cereza.*
   *¡Rabia, rabia, Marco Polo!*
*Sobre una fantástica rueda,*
*los niños ven lontananzas*
*desconocidas de la tierra.*
   *Corpus azul.*
*Blanca nochebuena.*

(Holidays travel
on wheels.
The merry-go-round
carries and leads them.
   Blue Corpus Christi.
White Christmas Eve.

.   .   .   .

   The merry-go-round turns
hung from a star.
Tulip from five
parts of the earth.
   On little horses
masked as panthers,

61

children consume the moon
as though it were a cherry.
   Rage, rage, Marco Polo!
On a fantastic wheel,
children see the earth's
undiscovered distances.
   Blue Corpus Christi.
White Christmas Eve.)

But there is an indication of Lorca's development in the emphasis he gives to a refined erotic and musical sensualism. The first aspect derives from his preoccupation with botanical phenomena, while the other is an outgrowth of an esthetic obsession with musical ideas which seeks equilibrium between form and imagination. In his poem "La Soltera en Misa" ("The Spinster at Mass"), he reveals the mysterious conjunction between sex and prayer through the images of bull and melon:

> Bajo el Moisés del incienso,
> adormecida.
>    Ojos de toro te miraban.
> Tu rosario llovía.
>    Con ese traje de profunda seda,
> no te mueves, Virginia.
>    Da los negros melones de tus pechos
> al rumor de la misa.


>    (Asleep under the Moses
> of the incense.
>    Bull eyes regarding you.
> Your rosary, raining.
>    In that dress of deep silk,
> Virginia, do not move.
>    Give the black melons of your breasts
> to the murmur of the mass.)

To each of his three poetic portraits of Verlaine, Jiménez, and Debussy, all of them musical sensualists, are appended shorter poems to Bacchus, Venus, and Narcissus, respectively. To Verlaine, he chants "la canción que nunca diré" ("the song I shall never sing"); to Jiménez, he sings of the "white infinite of snow, spikenard, and the salt pit"; and to Debussy, of the "reflection of quiet things" in which the shade seeks to keep the restive body. His musical imagination looks for some accord between classical Greek sensualism and the spirit of wild vegetable opulence in Andalusia. In this, he is again traversing the path of the Arabic poets whose metaphoric system was a development from the botanical to the human, to the immutable perfection of the mineral, and whose ideal was to mitigate a too largely self-revealing erotic pleasure by the Platonic sublimation of chastity. Sentimentality, that last rigidity of the heart, is alien to the pattern. Only through form and apparatus must language glean its ultimate perfection: sensual reality. Yet complete triumph in this direction is not achieved in *Canciones;* the design has not been fulfilled though the craftsman's ingenuity has grown considerably.

At the same time, Lorca has established a mine of dramatic material, pointed toward the more condensed form of the ballad in *Romancero Gitano,* and finally toward the drama in his second period. A whole section, for instance, is devoted to songs of the moon—the moon which is to become so intimate a symbol in *Bodas de Sangre.* A number of poems like "Suicidio" ("Suicide"), "Narciso" ("Narcissus"), "Desposorio" ("Betrothal"), "El Lagarto Está Llorando" ("The Lizard is Weeping"), and

63

the section "Eros con Bastón" ("Eros with a Baton") suggest the problems of self-love confounded by the world, the grief of child and animal confronted by death, and the woman who luxuriates in her sex, frustrating the chastened imagination. These are themes which later find dramatic resolution in plays like *Así Que Pasen Cinco Años* and *Amor de Don Perlimplín con Belisa en Su Jardín*.

The intention of these poems, in which the symbols of the larger drama of time and place and death are already fixed, is to find the instinctive life in the fertile things of nature surrounding the poet. For if this is found, not only will the form become clear but the conventions in which these objects have been treated and often abused by former poets will be successfully broken, and the mysterious primitive origins and movements rediscovered. Attaining this, the poet will find an idiom allowing him to create a theatre capable of delineating traditional themes with fresh implications. When Lorca becomes completely conscious of what he is able to do in poetry, he will find it possible to write drama. And this comes with *Romancero Gitano* and *Poeta en Nueva York*.

# 4. TRIUMPH OF SENSUAL REALITY— MATURE VERSE

*ROMANCERO GITANO (BOOK OF GYPSY BALLADS)* (1928) IS THE realization of poetic sensibility which has achieved technical mastery over its materials. Here the poet's restless imagination has at last found a form in which to cast his personal cosmology. Less slavish to the letter of folkloric devices, Lorca has begun to create a respectable folklore of his own. The characteristic concentration upon a theme in single monotone, which occurs in the conventional Andalusian song, is replaced in *Romancero Gitano* by a solid variety of thematic materials. These are elaborated in subtle musical patterns with a personal emphasis which marks the matured poetic spirit. Written in the traditional octosyllabic meter, these ballads become a series of re-invented *cantares de gesta.* They partake of the anonymous folk character upholding a tradition distinctive for its magical re-creation of language and its exaltation of natural phenomena and pagan feeling. Spanish poets beginning with Jiménez sought to eschew the anecdotal qualities of the old *romance* and to reshape the form according to new inventive techniques. And this is Lorca's first accomplishment in *Romancero Gitano*. He has re-created the classical style of the old ballad and given it a new tonal quality which is distinctly modern.

*Romancero Gitano* reflects the sorrows of a persecuted people living on the margins of society, who maintain their old tribal primitivism intact. Hounded by the police, their conflict is symbolized by the silver steel of their knives and the Mausers of the law. The Civil Guard which hunts them through the night pervades like a plague:

> *Los caballos negros son.*
> *Las herraduras son negras.*
> *Sobre las capas relucen*
> *manchas de tinta y de cera.*
> *Tienen, por eso no lloran,*
> *de plomo las calaveras.*
> *Con el alma de charol*
> *vienen por la carretera.*
> *Jorobados y nocturnos,*
> *por donde animan ordenan*
> *silencios de goma oscura*
> *y miedos de fina arena.*
> *Pasan, si quieren pasar,*
> *y ocultan en la cabeza,*
> *una vaga astronomía*
> *de pistolas inconcretas.*
>
> ( Black are their horses
> and black their horses' hooves.
> Upon their capes stains
> of ink and wax glisten.
> Because their skulls are made

66

of lead they do not weep.
With patent-leather souls
they come down the road.
Hunched and nocturnal,
wherever they stir they compel
silences of dark India rubber
and fears of fine sand.
They pass, if they wish to,
and hide in their heads
a vague astronomy
of indefinite pistols.)

The constant struggle of the gypsies is against a universal repression whose edict is death. They themselves, however, own the moon's proud body which they hammer on a forge in the intimacy of the surrounding night. A people whose innocence is as endless as their misery, they know no argument more final than the fatal message of the dark-winged angels:

*Una dura luz de naipe*
*recorta en el agrio verde*
*caballos enfurecidos*
*y perfiles de jinetes.*
*En la copa de un olivo*
*lloran dos viejas mujeres.*
*El toro de la reyerta*
*se sube por las paredes.*
*Ángeles negros traían*
*pañuelos y agua de nieve.*
*Ángeles con grandes alas*
*de navajas de Albacete.*
*Juan Antonio el de Montilla*
*rueda muerto la pendiente,*
*su cuerpo lleno de lirios,*
*y una granada en las sienes.*

**67**

*Ahora monta cruz de fuego,*
*carretera de la muerte.*

. . . . .

*La tarde loca de higueras*
*y de rumores calientes*
*cae desmayada en los muslos*
*heridos de los jinetes.*
*Y ángeles negros volaban*
*por el aire de poniente.*
*Ángeles de largas trenzas*
*y corazones de aceite.*

(A sharp light of cards
cuts into the bitter green
profiles of riders
and furious horses.
In the bower of an olive tree
two old women weep.
The bull of argument
climbs over the walls.
Black angels were bearing
scarves and water of snow.
Angels with huge wings
sheer as knives from Albacete.
Juan Antonio Montilla, dead,
is rolling down the slope,
his body full of lilies,
between his temples, a grenade.
Now a cross of fire mounts
the highway of death.

. . . . .

The afternoon, mad with fig trees
and warm murmuring,
faints in the horsemen's
wounded thighs.

And black angels were flying
through the west wind.
Angels with long tresses
and hearts of oil.)

Nothing sleeps where the gypsies ride; every image, every stone conceals some threat of danger. Thus, the wind itself suddenly grows lustful and chases Preciosa, the gypsy girl, clear down the mountains into the house of the English Consul. And the iconography of some obscure Byzantine retable depicting the martyrdom of Saint Eulalie is immediately transformed in the erotic symbolism of Lorca's balladry:

*Flor desnuda se sube*
*por escalerillas de agua.*
*El Cónsul pide bandeja*
*para los senos de Olalla.*
*Un chorro de venas verdes*
*le brota de la garganta.*
*Su sexo tiembla enredado*
*como un pájaro en las zarzas.*
*Por el suelo, ya sin norma,*
*brincan sus manos cortadas*
*que aún pueden cruzarse en tenue*
*oración decapitada.*
*Por los rojos agujeros*
*donde sus pechos estaban*
*se ven cielos diminutos*
*y arroyos de leche blanca.*

(A nude flower climbs
the water rack.
The Consul asks a tray
for the breasts of Eulalie.

**69**

A spurt of green veins
bursts from her throat.
Her sex trembles like a bird
caught in the brambles.
On the ground, now undisciplined,
leap her cut-off hands,
which can still cross themselves
in soft decapitated prayer.
Through red pin-holes
where were her breasts,
miniature skies
and milk white streams are seen.)

The austere agony of a Catholic martyr's death is turned
into a daylight-flushed scene of a bright little Roman orgy,
such as might appear commemorated on a Goya tapestry.
The same splendor of a re-animated Romanesque landscape permeates the ballads on the three Andalusian
saints, Michael, Raphael, and Gabriel:

San Miguel, lleno de encajes
en la alcoba de su torre,
enseña sus bellos muslos
ceñidos por los faroles.

. . . . .

Vienen manolas comiendo
semillas de girasoles,
los culos grandes y ocultos
como planetas de cobre.
Vienen altos caballeros
y damas de triste porte,
morenas por la nostalgia
de un ayer de ruiseñores.

(In his tower room, full of lace,
San Miguel displays
his handsome thighs
ringed by lantern light.

.        .        .

Fashionable wenches come eating
sunflower seeds,
their big hidden behinds
like copper planets.
Distinguished lords go by
and ladies sad in aspect,
dark-pale with longing
for a past of nightingales.)

Into each of these three ballads are woven the alternate patterns of background and the action of figures, while here and there a popular vignette is interspersed. Meanwhile, an entirely new geography has been created for the purpose, so that history itself stares out with sudden interest. It is as if a legend had been garnered from the past and a particular crystallized world invented through which a select species of plants and animals and peoples of every race in Andalusia might promenade. But the stylization of imagery which contains them is never utterly fixed as in Góngora. The secret of fluidity is revealed in the poet's own relentless pursuit of a nature which never finds its rest. Lorca's vision never betrays him into accepting a half-awakened reality as an ultimate form of permanence. This vision triumphs only when the poem has entered the province of song, and all artifice has been merged into the quick movement of feeling and rhythm. The stratagems he uses are attempts to construct an esthetic

**71**

frame that will at once dignify a people whose genius is so little understood and interpret their ancient spirit in modern form. The poet hopes to come upon a permanent facet of emotion, and perhaps thereby to define his own temperament more closely. In "La Casada Infiel" ("The Faithless Wife"), for example, he reveals the quiet essence of gypsy dignity which an innate eroticism can never completely overcome:

> Fué la noche de Santiago
> y casi por compromiso.
> Se apagaron los faroles
> y se encendieron los grillos.
> En las últimas esquinas
> toqué sus pechos dormidos,
> y se me abrieron de pronto
> como ramos de jacintos.
> El almidón de su enagua
> me sonaba en el oído
> como una pieza de seda
> rasgada por diez cuchillos.

> . . . . .

> Pasadas las zarzamoras,
> los juncos y los espinos,
> bajo su mata de pelo
> hice un hoyo sobre el limo.
> Yo me quité la corbata.
> Ella se quitó el vestido.
> Yo el cinturón con revólver.
> Ella sus cuatro corpiños.
> Ni nardos ni caracolas
> tienen el cutis tan fino,
> ni los cristales con luna
> relumbran con ese brillo.

*Sus muslos se me escapaban*
*como peces sorprendidos. . . .*

.    .    .    .    .

*No quiero decir, por hombre,*
*las cosas que ella me dijo.*
*La luz del entendimiento*
*me hace ser muy comedido.*
*Sucia de besos y arena*
*yo me la llevé del río.*

.    .    .    .    .

*Me porté como quien soy:*
*como un gitano legítimo.*
*Le regalé un costurero*
*grande, de raso pajizo,*
*y no quise enamorarme*
*porque teniendo marido*
*me dijo que era mozuela*
*cuando la llevaba al río.*

(It was on the night of St. James
and almost as if so arranged.
The streetlights were doused
and the crickets lit up.
On the outskirts of the town
I touched her sleeping breasts,
and they opened to me quickly
like a branch of hyacinths.
The starch of her petticoat
sounded in my ears
like a piece of silk
slashed by ten knives.

.    .    .    .    .

Past the bramble bushes,
the rushes and the thorns,

under her long, thick hair
I made a hollow in the mud.
I took off my tie.
She took off her dress.
I my revolver and belt.
She her four underwaists.
Not spikenard or snails
have skin so fine,
nor do moonlit crystals shine
with such brilliance.
Her thighs escaped me
like two fishes surprised.

.　　.　　.

As a man of honor, I won't divulge
the things she told me.
The light of understanding
has made me quite prudent.
Stained with kisses and sand,
I carried her from the river.

.　　.　　.

I behaved as I am:
a true gypsy.
I gave her a large sewing box
of straw-colored satin,
but did not intend to be her lover,
for though she had a husband
she told me she was a virgin
when I carried her to the river.)

It is an untutored spiritual grace by which the gypsy
lives. Like the tenth-century Arabic poet, he is cognizant
of the higher human ethic which keeps the abandoned
beast from entering the garden. The symbols of Arab and
Gypsy are both so intricately entwined in Lorca's sensi-

bility that it is not always possible to draw a comparative inference from the manner in which he treats either of them. However, one may perhaps differentiate between the more studied, decadent eroticism of the Arabic lover and the eroticism which rises as an earth-force to purify the gypsy. In the historical ballad "Thamár y Amnón," for example, Lorca presents an episode of incestuous love, a legend of Arabic imagination. Filled with such an intoxicating air of sensual vibrations, the poem suggests the depravity into which love falls when ethical discipline perverts the natural instinct:

> —Thamár, bórrame los ojos
> con tu fija madrugada.
> Mis hilos de sangre tejen
> volantes sobre tu falda.
> —Déjame tranquila, hermano.
> Son tus besos en mi espalda
> avispas y vientecillos
> en doble enjambre de flautas.
> —Thamár, en tus pechos altos
> hay dos peces que me llaman,
> y en las yemas de tus dedos
> rumor de rosa encerrada.
>
> .     .     .     .
>
> Alrededor de Thamár
> gritan vírgenes gitanas
> y otras recogen las gotas
> de su flor martirizada.
> Paños blancos enrojecen
> en las alcobas cerradas.
>
> .     .     .     .
>
> Violador enfurecido,
> Amnón huye con su jaca.

*Negros le dirigen flechas*
*en los muros y atalayas.*
*Y cuando los cuatro cascos*
*eran cuatro resonancias,*
*David, con unas tijeras,*
*cortó las cuerdas del arpa.*

(—Thamár, pluck out my eyes
with your fixed dawn.
Threads of my blood weave
flounces in your dress.
—Brother, let me be.
Your kisses on my shoulder
are wasps and little winds
in a double swarm of flutes.
—In your high breasts, Thamár,
two fishes are calling me,
and in the cushions of your fingers
the murmur of a hidden rose.

.    .    .    .    .

All about Thamár
the gypsy virgins wail,
while others receive the drops
of her martyrized flower.
White sheets turn red in
the closed bedrooms.

.    .    .    .    .

Amnón, the frightened seducer,
flees on his pony.
Negroes shoot darts
from the walls and ramparts.
And when the four hoofs
became four echoes,
David, with a pair of shears,
cut the strings of his harp.)

One folkloric quality of the ballads is their deep anonymity which cannot be easily plumbed; this is the very spring from which their emotional complex issues. It is not necessary to seek directly into the incidents of origin in order to build, as Lorca did, upon the old cultural structures. Lorca's use of the traditional ballad gradually merges with his whole esthetic procedure. This use is not the mere exploitation of a theme for the discursiveness of some folkloric poetaster; it is a marriage between the language of personal perception and the language of popular feeling. Lorca's esthetic demands continually enhance a subjective element of gypsy atmosphere in Andalusian life which others have overworked as an exotic attraction without particular spiritual significance. In *Romancero Gitano*, Lorca arrived at a unique synthesis between popular subject matter and his own artistic personality. He thereby came upon the main current of the Spanish tradition which unites the old with the new, the popular with the sophisticated, the lyrical with the narrative. But *Romancero Gitano* was in no sense a consummation of artistic purpose. Lorca's spirit was still hungry, as is the spirit of every poet who feels the burden of "the song I shall never sing." For Lorca was not interested in the popular elements of Andalusian culture alone. In his restless seeking of a bond between the habits of an older cultural perception and the values of the modern world, he felt compelled to experiment ceaselessly with different forms.

And so, some time during the years 1926–1929, Lorca wrote two odes in classical hexameters which are curiously beyond the range of anything he had done before. They

**77**

augur the strangely moving idiom of *Poeta en Nueva York*, and illuminate the quest for equilibrium between his already established modes of perception and the objective reality of the changing world outside Andalusia. The first poem, *Oda a Salvador Dalí*, is an attempt to celebrate not so much the art of his painter friend as Dalí's faith in the same world of the senses which Lorca was treating with quite a different organization of objective phenomena. Lorca sees the justice of isolating objects from their accepted surroundings, having attempted the same concentration in his own poetry; he feels it, in fact, the only way to give them that instinctive life which is their essence, and which otherwise is lost in the confusion and banality of massive, unmeaning landscapes surrounding them:

> *Los pintores modernos, en sus blancos estudios,*
> *cortan la flor aséptica de la raíz cuadrada.*

> *Un deseo de formas y límites nos gana.*

> *El mundo tiene sordas penumbras y desorden*
> *en los primeros terminos que el humano frecuenta.*

> *La corriente del tiempo se remansa y ordena*
> *en las formas numéricas de un siglo y otro siglo.*
> *Y la Muerte vencida se refugia temblando*
> *en el círculo estrecho del minuto presente.*

> *Amas una materia definida y exacta*
> *donde el hongo no pueda poner su campamento.*

# TRIUMPH OF SENSUAL REALITY—MATURE VERSE

*Pero también la rosa del jardín donde vives.*
*¡ Siempre la rosa, siempre, norte y sur de nosotros!*
*Tranquila y concentrada como una estatua ciega,*
*ignorante de esfuerzos soterrados que causa.*

*Rosa pura que limpia de artificios y croquis*
*y nos abre las alas tenues de la sonrisa.*
*( Mariposa clavada que medita su vuelo.)*
*Rosa del equilibrio sin dolores buscados.*
*¡ Siempre la rosa!*

*¡ Oh, Salvador Dalí de voz aceitunada!*
*Digo lo que me dicen tu persona y tus cuadros.*
*No alabo tu imperfecto pincel adolescente,*
*pero canto la firme dirección de tus flechas.*

*Canto tu bello esfuerzo de luces catalanas,*
*tu amor a lo que tiene explicación posible.*


(Modern painters in their white studios
cut the aseptic flower from the square root.

.    .    .    .    .    .    .    .    .

We are pleased by the instinct for form and discipline.

.    .    .    .    .    .    .    .    .

The world puts stifled penumbras and disorder
in the foreground where humanity crowds.

.    .    .    .    .    .    .    .    .

Time's flow is stopped and ordered
in the numerical forms of century after century.
And trembling, vanished Death seeks refuge
in the narrow circle of the present moment.

.    .    .    .    .    .    .    .    .

You love matter defined and exact
where fungus can make no lodging.

. . . . . . .

But also the rose in the garden where you live.
Always the rose, always, north and south of us!
Calm and concentrated as a blind statue,
unconscious of underground forces which push it up.

Pure rose, clean of artifice and mere approximation,
opening for us the delicate wings of the smile.
(Pinned-up butterfly contemplating flight.)
Rose of equilibrium hunting no sorrows.
Always the rose!

O, Salvador Dalí, voice steeped in olives!
I speak of what your person and your art tell me.
I praise not your imperfect adolescent brush,
but sing the firm direction of your arrows.

I sing your handsome energy full of Catalan light,
your love of what has a possible explanation.)

Whether one agrees with Lorca that the art of Salvador
Dalí indicates such a "firm direction" is probably not
fundamental. What is important is that Lorca, who has
been called the "unconscious" artist *par excellence*, could
identify himself in the cosmic vision of the new art which
Dalí represented. In some sense every artist is concerned
with rearranging his landscape, both within and without.
But rarely can one express effectively, as Lorca does here,
the consciousness of so shadowy a purpose.

The second hexameter poem, "Oda al Santísimo Sacramento del Altar: Exposición y Mundo" ("Ode to the Most
Holy Eucharist: Exposition and World"), is still another

**80**

aspect of the same esthetic principle. Lorca perceives in the form of the Eucharist the living Christ as a concrete expression of man's agony. But it is not an heroic figure he sees; it is a Christ made diminutive as a doll—the figure which Spanish children carry about on Christmas and Easter—or it is a Christ as small and palpitating as a frog's heart which doctors place in a bell jar:

> Es así, Dios andado, como quiero tenerte.
> Panderito de harina para el recién nacido.
> Brisa y materia juntas en expresión exacta
> por amor de la carne que no sabe tu nombre.
>
> Es así, forma breve de rumor inefable,
> Dios en mantillas, Cristo diminuto y eterno,
> repetido mil veces, muerto, crucificado
> por la impura palabra del hombre suderoso.
>
> .    .    .    .    .    .    .    .
>
> ¡Oh, Forma sacratísima, vértice de las flores,
> donde todos los ángulos toman sus luces fijas,
> donde número y boca construyen un presente
> cuerpo de luz humana con músculos de harina!
>
> ¡Oh, Forma limitada para expresar concreta
> muchedumbre de luces y clamor escuchado!
> ¡Oh, nieve circundada por témpanos de música!
> ¡Oh, llama crepitante sobre todas las venas!

> (Thus would I have you, familiar God.
> Little flour wafer for the new-born child.
> Wind and substance joined in exact expression
> by love for the flesh which knows not your name.
>
> In such a way, concise form of ineffable sound,
> God in infant's dress, diminutive, eternal Christ,

**81**

a thousand times pronounced dead, crucified
by the impure word of sweaty man.

   .    .    .    .    .    .    .

Oh, most holy Form, apex of the flowers,
where all angles take their fixed lights,
where mouth and number construct a body's offering
of human light and muscles of flour!

Oh, Form limited to express a concrete
multitude of lights and heeded din!
Oh, snow bounded by timbrels of music!
Oh, flame crackling over all our veins!)

In the outer world, such a form is constantly overcome
by cruelty and murder symbolized by the razor lying on
the table and avidly waiting to slit the throat. In that
world, "three thousand men came armed with shining
knives to assassinate the nightingale."—

> *Noche de rostro blanco. Nula noche sin rostro.*
> *Bajo el Sol y la Luna. Triste noche del Mundo.*
> *Dos mitades opuestas y un hombre que no sabe*
> *cuando su mariposa dejará los relojes.*
>
>    .    .    .    .    .    .
>
> *Sólo tu Sacramento de luz en equilibrio,*
> *aquietaba la angustia del amor desligado.*
>
>    .    .    .    .    .    .
>
> *Porque tu signo es clave de llanura celeste.*
>
>    .    .    .    .    .    .
>
> *Porque tu signo expresa la brisa y el gusano.*
> *Punto de unión y cita del siglo y minuto.*
>
> *Mundo, ya tienes meta para tu desamparo.*
> *Para tu horror perenne de agujero sin fondo.*

# TRIUMPH OF SENSUAL REALITY—MATURE VERSE

*¡Oh, Cordero cautivo de tres voces iguales!*
*¡Sacramento inmutable de amor y disciplina!*

(White-faced night. Night void and characterless.
Under the Sun and Moon. Sad night of the World.
Two halves opposed and a man who does not know
when his butterfly will leave the clocks.

     .     .     .     .     .     .

Only your balanced Sacrament of light
pacified the anguish of unloosed love.

    .     .     .     .     .     .     .

Because your sign is a key to the celestial plain.

    .     .     .     .     .     .

Because your sign expresses the wind and the worm.
Appointed meeting place of century and moment.

World, you now have a goal for your helplessness.
For your perennial horror of the bottomless hole.
O, captive Lamb of three equal voices!
Immutable Sacrament of love and discipline!)

Just as Lorca discovered in Dalí's art a courageous instinct to deal with phenomena of pure form, so in the
body and spirit of Christ he found committed the "love
and discipline" by which he also sought to implement his
poetry.

For Lorca, the Holy Eucharist was the religious counterpart of his own esthetic; in the unity of the godhead
was the same concretization of form symbolized. Through
this unity one might aspire to find "love and discipline"
outside the characterless flux of the world. Lorca was not
seeking to dehumanize experience—a fatal thing for a

**83**

poet—but to attempt some imaginative expression which his former treatment of sensual reality did not admit.

It is interesting to note that in a letter written to a fellow-poet during this time, Lorca speaks of his Odes as spiritual exercises, as attempts to overcome a sense of artistic irresolution and personal despair. He counsels his friend, by his own example, not to allow "these ugly things" to infiltrate his poetry, "because [they] will play you the trick of revealing what is purest in you to the eyes of those who should *never* see it. For that reason, and as a discipline, I am now composing these precise *exercises* and opening my soul to the symbol of the Eucharist. . . ." And in another letter concerning the Odes Lorca adds, "I am now writing a kind of *opening-the-veins* poetry, a poetry altogether *averted* from reality, with a feeling which reflects all my love for things and all my *mocking* of things. Love of death and poking fun at it." Yet he also remarks with decision, "After finishing my Odes, in which I have placed so much illusion, I shall close this poetic cycle to turn toward something else." When Lorca describes this poetry as "averted" from reality, reflecting his love of death and his poking fun at it, he makes the strangely pertinent admission of a personality suggesting less the conscientious artist than the sharp wisdom of the peasant. It was this certainty of instinct which preserved for Lorca his cultural roots in Spain, though he sought momentarily the deepening of death's mystery in a foreign landscape completely outside his knowledge. This new attempt might easily have come as a reaction to the localized experience of *Poema del Cante Jondo* and *Romancero Gitano*. Whether it was impatience with what seemed a too easy accomplishment in his field or the fear of repeating himself, there was already impetus enough to prepare him for the strange world of New York. Only later was he to realize, however, that discarding the known aspects of localism for the unknown aspects of the universal is but another way of dealing with the same problem.

Lorca's short stay in New York resulted in the volume *Poeta en Nueva York*. It is the work of a new spiritual insight and of a largely incoherent prophetic vision. Tormented and mutilated, but still sensually realistic, the poems included in this volume carry a peculiarly important message to the modern age. It is easy to think of them as the fabrications of a mind which has lost its balance, as the outpourings of a surrealist gruesomely constructing an anti-human nightmare world. Certainly they are Lorca's most difficult poems. Musically discordant, disrupted in meter, poured into an arbitrary autonomous form, cascading with the fragments of exploded metaphor, they seem to contradict the whole of his previous procedure. But their secret is that a new world of imagery has been created to embody the fervid spiritual effort which informs them. The intricate imagistic and metaphoric terminology of *Poeta en Nueva York* proceeds from a vision of the world which, finding no expressive instrument in the traditions of any communicative medium, demands of the poet a new imaginative invention.

Begun on a note of spiritual defeat ("Murdered by heaven/ between the forms that issue towards the serpent/ and the forms that seek the crystal . . ."), which is still the poet's concern with form and his sense of failure in the struggle to attain it, Lorca drives relentlessly through the metropolitan jungle to emerge with a song of biological renewal in the rhythm of a Cuban chant, the *son*. Thus, what begins as the denunciation of a civilization which has repudiated all natural form, gradually grows into a paean glorifying the instincts of the one race in the New World—the Negro—that has never relinquished such a form. Meanwhile, livid as a scar are the impressions conveyed of the poet's reawakened vision of death, his refuge in a primitive Christ, and a profound Catholic sentiment, which is at the same time a bitter condemnation of the Church of Rome. *Poeta en Nueva York* includes Lorca's finest mystic expression in the same spirit of religious heresy which has always made Spain more Catholic than the letter of the Church's dogma could warrant. Thus Lorca's incongruent language becomes the very instrument with which a deep spiritual unity is sought. It takes on the indefinable quality of all Spanish mysticism: the knowledge of roots deep in the soil, flowering into human integration. It is the unifying element in a work which rises above the equivocations of poetic analysis in its triumphant surrender to the chaos of the modern world.

The insomnia which would not allow the poet to shut his eye to any moment in Granada is transmuted in New York into the fear of death, the fear that what is precious in each passing moment will be eternally lost as soon as one has allowed himself the luxury of believing that the flux has stopped. There is no way for man to escape into a haven of exalted reality, a quickening of the spirit such as Calderón, for example, envisioned in heaven. No. Those who sleep are blinding themselves to the death and perversity which is man's own creation:

> No duerme nadie por el mundo. Nadie, nadie.
> Ya lo he dicho.
> No duerme nadie.
> Pero si alguien tiene por la noche exceso de musgo en las sienes,
> abrid los escotillones para que vea bajo la luna
> las copas falsas, el veneno y la calavera de los teatros.

> (Nobody in the world is sleeping. Nobody.
> I've said so.
> Nobody is sleeping.
> But if someone at night has excessive moss at the temples,
> open the trapdoors so he may see under the moon
> the theatres' false goblets, the poison, and the skull.)

For Lorca, New York is a symbol of spiritual myopia, where man is unable to cope with the disease of body and soul because he cannot see the nature of his dislocation, because he has lost sight of those elemental natural forces which a people living close to the soil understand instinctively. Here men use the wrong "juices," and flail themselves with their nerves until they stumble into the arms of the devil—or what is still more probable, some psychoanalyst. Behind the surge of marching facts and gigantically misspent energies, the poet sees the agony close to the bone, the cancer creeping through the body; he is aware of no salvation and can discern only the wound from which half of humanity must die. At such moments he speaks more clearly, as clearly as Christ spoke to His disciples at the Last Supper, when there is no ter-

**87**

ror of confused panoramas to haunt his eyes, when he is cleansed by the meaning of his own life:

> Yo denuncio a toda la gente
> que ignora la otra mitad,
> la mitad irredimible
> que levanta sus montes de cemento
> donde laten los corazones
> de los animalitos que se olvidan
> y donde caeremos todos
> en la última fiesta de los taladros.
> Os escupo en la cara.
> La otra mitad me escucha
> devorando, orinando, volando, en su pureza. . . .

> (I denounce all those
> who ignore the other half,
> the irredeemable half
> raising mountains of cement
> where beat the hearts
> of little forgotten beasts
> and where we shall all tumble
> on the last holiday of the blast charges.
> I spit in your face.
> The other half hears me
> devouring, urinating, flying, in its purity. . . .)

With Lorca, Death is always a silent wanderer. In his earlier poems Death appears as a monolithic force which triumphantly overwhelms life because there is no opposition. In *Poeta en Nueva York,* everything falsely believed is Death: a thing created by a tradition of incomprehension and blindness. Like the proverbial old beggar woman, it endures because it is so implicitly accepted. In the poem "Danza de la Muerte" ("Dance of Death"), Death carries a mask; but behind the mask is the face of a Negro, who, for Lorca, has a special significance in America: a race apart, martyred for its ceremonial purity and primal innocence. Thus, by a curious inversion, the very incarnation of life comes behind the mask of death to liberate humanity. What lives and moves with the earth is the rhythm of the Negro's blood. He alone does not need to learn the secret of nature's flux; only he, bound by a civilization of steel nerves, knows the music and dance of passion which is eternal:

> ¡Ay Harlem! ¡Ay Harlem! ¡Ay Harlem!
> ¡No hay augustia comparable a tus ojos oprimidos,
> a tu sangre estremecida dentro del eclipse obscuro,
> a tu violencia granate sordomuda en la penumbra,
> a tu gran rey prisionero, con un traje de conserje!

> (Ay, Harlem, Harlem, Harlem!
> There is no sorrow like your oppressed eyes,
> like your blood shuddering in the dark eclipse,
> your garnet violence, deaf in shadow and dumb,
> like your great king, prisoner in a janitor's uniform.)

For the Negro, the Jew, the Gypsy, the poor; for races and classes as old as the earth, who must taste the gall of poverty and agony and must learn how to suffer; for all these Lorca has an affection which, in proof, is greater than for his Granadine gardens. It is "this other half" that teaches the poet the meaning of his own life, the pain of the searching, unconsummated spirit. And Lorca does find one man in America who expresses the purity and realistic love of the senses. His is the primitive voice: a voice of dignity, conscious and dreaming, in whose compass all that is false must die. He walked the streets of this same New York, and while "no one wanted to be a cloud," and while "no one wanted to be a river," or to love "the great leaves" and the "beach's blue tongue," he paused to become everything he saw. He is the "hidden angel," the "perfect voice" that will "tell the truth of the wheat" in a New York of "wires and death." He is Walt Whitman.

> *Ni un solo momento, viejo hermoso Walt Whitman,*
> *he dejado de ver tu barba llena de mariposas,*
> *ni tus hombros de pana gastados por la luna,*
> *ni tus muslos de Apolo virginal,*
> *ni tu voz como una columna de ceniza;*
> *anciano hermoso como la niebla*
> *que gemías igual que un pájaro*
> *con el sexo atravesado por una aguja,*
> *enemigo del sátiro,*
> *enemigo de la vid,*
> *y amante de los cuerpos bajo la burda tela.*

> (Not for one moment, handsome old Walt Whitman,
> have I forgotten your beard full of butterflies,
> or your corduroy shoulders worn by the moon,
> or your thighs of virginal Apollo,
> or your voice like a column of ashes;
> old man, beautiful as the mist,
> trembling like a bird
> whose sex is pierced by a needle,
> enemy of the satyr,
> enemy of the vine,
> and lover of bodies under the coarse fabric.)

Though a stranger to the scene, Lorca identifies himself with the burly American poet. Obsessed with the same sense of the body's purity, he rises to the greatest pitch of condemnation in his "Oda a Walt Whitman"; for having discovered the purest fruit, he has recognized the worm of perversion eating at its core. Freaks, contortionists of the senses, frauds representing every degree of physiological and psychological disease—they obliterate nature and fill the blood with poison. Through them the world becomes a stark dream of frustration and death, and the spirit, a little limping thing which cries under a hot leaf in the jungle:

> *Agonía, agonía, sueño, fermento y sueño.*
> *Este es el mundo, amigo, agonía, agonía.*
> *Los muertos se descomponen bajo el reloj de las ciudades,*
> *la guerra pasa llorando con un millón de ratas grises,*
> *los ricos dan a sus queridas*
> *pequeños moribundos iluminados*
> *y la vida no es noble, ni buena, ni sagrada.*

> (Agony, agony, dream, ferment and dream.
> This is the world, my friend, agony, agony.
> The dead are rotting under the city clocks.
> War goes by weeping with a million grey rats;
> rich men give their mistresses
> tiny dying illuminati,
> and life is not noble, or good, or sacred.)

Caught up with all these are also those who might be lovers, who burn but cannot escape; those innocents, those "recluses of casinos who bitterly drink the water of prostitution;/ those of green glance who love man and burn their lips in silence." They will go down, guiltless, to the same death of the perverts, for their voices have been robbed. Only when the killers of the innocent have been denied will there be a new primeval dawn, when

**91**

man will come upon the first glories of himself and the New World.

Lorca's Catholicism as seen through his "Oda a Walt Whitman" is supremely a thing of the body, a touchstone for the mystic singing body. Viewing the city as a Babylon of false tongues, Lorca insisted on upholding a primitive Christianity. Often his language reverts to the symbolism of the Mass, and to the rhythm of the Christian chant; but it is only the more to prove that the traditional dogma is meaningless here where the first demands of the spirit are scarcely understood. The earth, bread, fire, water, and blood, the nutriments of life without which it is impossible to understand love, have all gone under the hill with the ants. The killer perseveres and his victims are legion. This is Lorca's argument; this is the essential Lorca risen from his struggle with the music and air of the Granadine gardens to hunt the hunter in the jungle of New York.

Fortunately, Lorca had not cut off his own retreat. It was still possible for him to rediscover the localism of Andalusia, from which he had momentarily rebelled, a stronger and more conscious artist. After the cosmic vision of *Poeta en Nueva York,* he was ready to appraise his earlier materials, and to intensify his cultural perception. This was done, after the return to Spain, in his drama and in two significant poetic works.

Shortly before his death in 1936, Lorca was revising a collection of poems which he intended for publication under the title *El Diván del Tamarit* (*The Diván at the Tamarit*). Although some of these appeared in magazines and anthologies (and more recently, reprinted in Angel del Río's study of Lorca), they are still an unedited work.

The insight they provide into Lorca's last stage as a poet is of outstanding importance. The poems reflect Lorca's reinstatement in the land of his birth. They are a re-affirmation of the cultural heritage he had gained from the medieval Arabic poets, and they celebrate again the esthetic of sensual form in fleeting time, characteristic of the best Arabic issue in Andalusia. *El Diván del Tamarit* renews the attempt to capture the sound and meaning of the spirit's warfare with nature in Andalusia: a land where life and death have only the few disguises which every object, animate or inanimate, alternately has put on and taken off each day for over a thousand years.

The *Tamarit* was the chief administrative office of Arabic power in Spain during the period of Moorish domination. The *Diván* was the Arabic name for the assembly of governors who came periodically to hold council with the *Tamarit*. *Diván* also has another meaning: "reunion." And it is probably in this sense that Lorca intended it.[1] By celebrating the spirit of all southern Spain, he sought to come to a "reunion" with his past.

They are poems of sheer imagistic delicacy, in the style of the *gacela* and *casida,* two standard Arabic verse forms used for love poetry and Anacreontic odes. The poems in *El Diván del Tamarit* comprising the bulk of the *gacelas* sing of a love no longer incarnate, which is beautiful in escape, mystic in remembered passion:

> *Nadie comprendía el perfume*
> *de la oscura magnolia de tu vientre.*

[1] It is probable that Lorca was also thinking of *Diván* in still another of its meanings—that of an "anthology" or "collection of poems."

*Nadie sabía que martirizabas*
*un colibrí de amor entre los dientes.*

*Mil caballitos persas se dormían*
*en la plaza con luna de tu frente,*
*mientras que yo enlazaba cuatro noches*
*tu cintura, enemiga de la nieve.*

*Entre yeso y jazmines, tu mirada*
*era un pálido ramo de simientes.*
*Yo busqué, para darte, por mi pecho*
*las letras de márfil que dicen* siempre.

Siempre, siempre: *jardín de mi agonía,*
*tu cuerpo fugitivo para siempre,*
*la sangre de tus venas en mi boca,*
*tu boca ya sin luz para mi muerte.*


(Nobody understood the perfume
of your belly's dark magnolia.
Nobody knew how you tormented
a humming bird of love between your teeth.

A thousand Persian ponies fell asleep
in the moonlit plaza of your forehead,
while four nights long I embraced
your waist, enemy of snow.

Between plaster and jasmin,
your glance was a pale seed branch.
I sought to give you from my heart
the ivory letters saying *always*.

*Always, always:* garden of my agony,
your blood fleeing forever,
blood of your veins in my mouth,
your mouth now unlit for my death.)

# TRIUMPH OF SENSUAL REALITY—MATURE VERSE

Lorca adopts the conventions although he does not maintain the old imagistic standards. He has already perfected his own. He adds to the Arabic theme a heightened sense of sympathy with the mineral, botanical, and animal worlds which create the immortal conflict in a nature too perfect to be stable:

> La rosa
> no buscaba la aurora:
> casi eterna en su ramo,
> buscaba otra cosa.
>
> La rosa
> no buscaba ni ciencia ni sombra:
> confín de carne y sueño,
> buscaba otra cosa.
>
> La rosa
> no buscaba la rosa.
> Inmóvil por el cielo
> buscaba otra cosa.

> (The rose
> did not seek the dawn:
> almost eternal on its branch,
> it sought another thing.
>
> The rose
> did not seek science or shadow:
> margin of flesh and dream,
> it sought another thing.
>
> The rose
> did not seek the rose.
> Motionless in the sky,
> it sought another thing.)

Hidden in the very being of the real rose are the destructive energies of transience by which nature turns it to decay. Reminiscent of "Oda a Salvador Dalí" ("always the rose, always, north and south of us," "aseptic," a pure form), the rose here attains the same plasticity which the Arabic poets used when they petrified it or turned it into a jewel. Lorca proposed for the undying, permutated rose an ideal counterpart in the human emotion, which though susceptible to decay may conserve its images of desire through "love and discipline." But if his poetry thus turns the external landscape into a solidified image of the inner landscape where all emotion has been depersonalized, it is not the typical romantic anthropomorphism. Lorca knew the rich possibilities which the use of certain limited concrete symbols afforded. He knew that once these became the poet's property, all desire could be poured into them as into a bottomless well if no cessation and no fulfillment were ever expected in the flow. Having appropriated these symbols, Lorca can dispose of the implications of cause and result. This is intentional and should not make the poems seem incomplete; rather, it suggests a vision which endures as an intimate companion of natural flux, and which, as a result, can never lie about the beginning and end of things. Desire becomes the one means of perpetuating all emotion; and emotion itself, serving as a universal human continuant, may vie with the unending tide of increase and decline in nature. In such a manner, death never stands out as a negative passion, but as part of a larger interminable experience which endures, because it is human, as long as any rock or tree endures, or as long as there are men to feel. There are abundance and extravagance in these poems because there is such abundance and extravagance in nature. And like the Arabic poets, Lorca created substance as rich as anything in nature.

This unusual harmony in Lorca's vision was re-inforced when, on the occasion of the death of the bullfighter Sánchez Mejías, his close friend, Lorca wrote what is perhaps his most sustained single poem: *Llanto por Ignacio Sánchez Mejías* (*Lament for Ignacio Sánchez Mejías*). He combined the lyrical devices of his earlier poems with the narrative devices of the historical ballad, and used the rhythm of the gypsy lament to carry the emotional impact of the tragedy. It is an admirable elegiac construction divided into four parts, whose individual motifs are fused in the manner of a Bach oratorio.

In the first section, "La Cogida y la Muerte" ("The Fatal Wound and the Death"), he announces the tragedy with an insistent refrain in every other line, recalling the hour in which the death took place: "at five in the afternoon." It is like a doleful bell rung out to the monotonous chant of a priest. It is an impersonal background to the death, where the wind bears away the shroud and the dove struggles with the leopard: the conflict of one form with another for ascendancy, of life with death, of spirit with matter. Then, as if viewed from above, the corpse of the bullfighter is seen lying in a coffin on wheels, the sound of bones and flutes in his ears, and the bull bellowing against his forehead.

In the second section, "La Sangre Derramada" ("The

Spilt Blood"), the death is described with time and space symbols through which the bullfighter sought to find a spiritual form:

> Por las gradas sube Ignacio
> con toda su muerte a cuestas.
> Buscaba el amanecer,
> y el amanecer no era.
> Busca su perfil seguro,
> y el sueño lo desorienta.
> Buscaba su hermoso cuerpo
> y encontró su sangre abierta.

> (Ignacio climbs the stairs
> carrying death on his shoulders.
> He sought the dawn
> and found it gone.
> He seeks his sharp profile
> and the dream cuts him off.
> He sought his handsome body
> and found his blood wide-opened.)

The poet calls on all things white to help him avoid seeing the blood spilled on the sand. "¡Que no quiero verla!" ("For I don't want to see it!") —

> Dile a la luna que venga,
> que no quiero ver la sangre
> de Ignacio sobre la arena.

> .    .    .    .    .

> ¡Avisad a los jazmines
> con su blancura pequeña!

> La vaca del viejo mundo
> pasaba su triste lengua

98

*sobre un hocico de sangres*
*derramadas en la arena,*
*y los toros de Guisando,*
*casi muerte y casi piedra,*
*mugieron como dos siglos*
*hartos de pisar la tierra.*
*No.*
*¡Que no quiero verla!*

(Tell the moon to come
for I don't want to see the blood
of Ignacio on the sand.

.        .        .        .

Tell the jasmins
in their small whiteness!

The cow of the old world
passed her sad tongue
over a snout of blood
spilt in the sand,
and the prehistoric bulls of Guisando,
made half of death, half of stone,
bellowed like two centuries
tired of treading the earth.
No.
I don't want to see it!)

The rhythm mounts slowly until it is cut by the refrain, in the manner of a guitar suddenly struck on the strings with the thumb. Then caught again on the same note and in the same tempo, it continues to rise and fall like quick, heavy breathing. During the pauses, Ignacio is compared in majesty and strength to a prince, an expert mountaineer, and to a "river of lions":

99

*No hubo príncipe en Sevilla*
*que comparársele pueda,*
*ni espada como su espada*
*ni corazón tan de veras.*
*Como un río de leones*
*su maravillosa fuerza,*
*y como un torso de mármol*
*su dibujada prudencia.*
*Aire de Roma andaluza*
*le doraba la cabeza*
*donde su risa era un nardo*
*de sal y de inteligencia.*

(There was not a prince like him in Seville
with whom comparison is possible,
nor any sword like his sword,
nor any heart so well endowed.
His miraculous courage
like a river of lions,
and like a sculptured torso
his dignity was hewn.
An air of Andalusian
Rome lit his head with gold
where his smile was a spikenard
of wit and of skill.)

When the obsession with spilt blood returns, the lines again are plucked like strings in the quick agony of the lament:

*¡Que no quiero verla!*
*Que no hay cáliz que la contenga,*
*que no hay golondrinas que se la beban,*
*no hay escarcha de luz que la enfríe,*
*no hay canto ni diluvio de azucenas,*
*no hay cristal que la cubra de plata.*

*No.*
*¡¡Yo no quiero verla!!*

(I don't want to see it!
For there is no chalice to contain it,
no swallows to drink it,
no frost of light to freeze it,
there is no song or flood of lilies
or mirror to cover it with silver.
No.
I don't want to see it!)

In the third section, "Cuerpo Presente" ("The Body in State"), the poet seems to detach himself from the scene and from the agony of the death. It is as though, in the previous section, he had experienced the death himself, the actual dying, as though he had been inside looking out. Now, however, he is outside looking in. The music of the verse becomes slow and speculative: a fourteen-syllable quatrain adapted to a melodic long line. It expresses a mystical time-space feeling sublimating the corpse into a symbol of all who are mortally injured and of all the exhausted continuity of human transience. Only that murderous solid, the self-repeating constant which is the stone, can endure death:

*La piedra es una espalda para llevar el tiempo*
*con árboles de lágrimas y cintas y planetas.*

*Yo he visto lluvias grises correr hacia las olas,*
*levantando sus tiernos brazos acribillados,*
*para no ser cazadas por la piedra tendida*
*que desata sus miembros sin empapar la sangre.*

**101**

(The stone is a shoulder to carry time
with trees of tears and ribbons and planets.

I have seen gray rains run toward the waves,
raising their tender perforated arms
in order not to be hunted by the outstretched stone
which unties their limbs without absorbing the blood.)

And now death has come to put Ignacio behind the stone, to shrink his humanity into the head of a minotaur. "Ya se acabó." ("It is finished.") The rain and the mad air, love full of frozen tears may stream over him, but he has become the victim of the stone—the body lying still under the white shroud. Yet the poet cannot accept physical death. The vision of man's perfection, his dominance over the flux of time and space must provide the secret of some exit behind the stone—a spiritual permanence:

> *Yo quiero ver aquí los hombres de voz dura.*
> *Los que doman caballos y dominan los ríos:*
> *los hombres que les suena el esqueleto y cantan*
> *con una boca llena de sol y pedernales.*
>
> *Aquí quiero yo verlos. Delante de la piedra.*
> *Delante de este cuerpo con las riendas quebradas.*
> *Yo quiero que me enseñen dónde está la salida*
> *para este capitán atado por la muerte.*

(I want to see men with rough voices here.
Those who tame horses and train rivers:
men whose bones ring out, who sing
with mouths full of sun and flint.

I want to see them here. Before the stone.
Before this body with broken reins.
I want them to show me the exit
for this captain bound by death.)

For what is death after all but a spiritual freedom from the customary bellowing of the death-instructed bull? Is man any less eternal than the sea, the sea which "also dies"?

> No quiero que le tapen la cara con pañuelos
> para que se acostumbre con la muerte que lleva.
> Vete, Ignacio: no sientas el caliente bramido.
> Duerme, vuela, reposa: ¡también se muere el mar!

> (I don't want them to bind his face in shrouds
> accustoming him to the death he carries.
> Forward, Ignacio: never mind the warm bellowing.
> Sleep, fly, rest: the sea also dies!)

Man's spirit may and does conquer death, as it conquers time and space, not because an afterlife has been created as a last refuge, but because Man has left the impression of his spiritual grace on earth where anyone with eyes to see may grasp it, may sing and celebrate and repeat it.

This is the argument of the fourth section, "Alma Ausente" ("The Soul in Absence"). Those who still need to be fed by the fluxional energies of life, who can believe only what passes and shoots before the eyes—they will not remember. They will forget the spirit of Ignacio as they forget the dead all over the earth, dying like "snuffed-out dogs."—

> No te conoce el toro ni la higuera,
> ni caballos ni hormigas de tu casa.
> No te conoce el niño ni la tarde
> porque te has muerto para siempre.

> No te conoce el lomo de la piedra,
> ni el raso negro donde te destrozas.

**103**

*No te conoce tu recuerdo mudo*
*porque te has muerto para siempre.*

(Neither the bull nor the fig tree knows you,
nor horses nor your household ants.
Neither child nor afternoon knows you
for you are forever dead.

Neither the stone's back nor the black satin
of your mangling knows you.
Nor does your silent memory know you
for you are forever dead.)

No one will remember but those, like the poet, who can lift the seal of mortality, who can look behind the stone, who can fix in the spirit's memory the crystal gaze of human grace and beauty, courage and appetite for death— the achievement of permanent form:

*Tardará mucho tiempo en nacer, si es que nace,*
*un andaluz tan claro, tan rico de aventura.*
*Yo canto su elegancia con palabras que gimen*
*y recuerdo una brisa triste por los olivos.*

(Long will it be before time yields, if ever it does,
an Andalusian as bright, as full of adventure.
I sing his grace with moaning words
and remember a sad breeze through the olive trees.)

*Llanto por Ignacio Sánchez Mejías* is the work of a poet in whose consciousness dramatic and poetic forms have interpenetrated. Even the manner of the poem's division into four parts, each carrying a different imaginative perspective on the death, suggests the architectural pattern of a play. The elaboration of a musical design within the poetic conception; the capture of the quality of *cante jondo* and the refinement of its basic rhythms in the verse; the coordination between narrative-episodic and lyric-elegiac forms; the consistency in the use of symbols—blood, bull, stone, body, sea, animals and trees—to contain as well as to depersonalize the huge impact of death; in all this one sees artifice merged into the imaginative projection itself, and the search for equilibrium become the very substance of dramatic incident and resolution. To appreciate the full dramatic consciousness which Lorca reached in *Llanto por Ignacio Sánchez Mejías,* one must turn to the work he had for some time been doing concurrently in the drama.

# 5. POET ON THE STAGE—DRAMATIC EXPERIMENTS

THE DRAMA OF SPAIN IS DISTINCT IN ORIGIN AND DEVELOP-
ment from any other in Europe. During the Golden Age
(1500–1700), the art of the written word grew from the
obscure, anonymous ballad collection to an expression in
poetry, novel and drama rivalling its lusty English counterpart of the Elizabethan Age. In both Spain and England, the genius of the age was popular, and not courtly
or pseudo-classical as in France and Italy. Because Spain's
most significant drama was rooted in the language of the
people, it early expressed a unified national culture. The
best work of the Golden Age is characterized by a spontaneity of idiom and a daring metaphoric quality. Its
themes are seldom divorced from common knowledge,
for literary men found little need to work outside the field
of popular experience. Working within this experience,
they were often able to dispense with the formalities of
logical structure, and by rich variations on traditional

patterns to strike immediately the same cultural recognition in all audiences however dissimilar.

As a direct outgrowth of the popular language and themes of traditional balladry, Spanish drama, differing in this sense from the English, quickly found its characteristic forms. As early as the mid-fifteenth century, a little Christmas piece, *Representación de Nuestro Señor*, ties up its dramatic consequences with a popular ballad sung at the end by a chorus of nuns. A little later, Juan del Encina developed the possibilities of combining song and recitation in his pastoral and religious plays—a device which gradually became respectable through the efforts of other early playwrights like Lucas Fernández and Gil Vicente, till it finally blossomed into Calderón's *zarzuela* (*music drama*). The tumultuous farces and religious *autos* (*allegories*) of Gil Vicente are alive with characters whose feet are aching to dance, whose voices at every turn are breaking into inspired song. In developing the *paso* (*curtain-raiser*), Lope de Rueda took the dramatic company into the yards and squares of the Spanish town. Though his poetic fancy hardly thrived with the same primitive energy as Gil Vicente's, his peasant characters admirably expressed the popular idiom of the day. Finally, by the time Juan de la Cueva evolved the *entremés* (*farce between-acts*), a strong national sentiment had invaded the theatre; the legendary heroes of Spain walked across the stage and the whole rich treasury of ballad literature was opened to exploitation. Thus, before the gargantuan output of the Golden Age, all the materials and techniques of Spanish national drama were already implicit in its structure. It was only left for Lope de Vega to perfect

**107**

the form of the ballad on the stage, and for Calderón de la Barca to give to the drama that spirit of speculation and faith which was the heart of the Spanish religious obsession through the Middle Ages and the Renaissance.

Spain's greatest drama before García Lorca was written by such Golden Age dramatists as Lope de Vega and Calderón de la Barca. And, inevitably, in trying to understand Lorca's appeal one recalls these figures separated from him by three centuries rather than his own contemporaries or near-contemporaries. Both Lope and Calderón spoke to a people whose lives were unified by Catholicism and by a sense of pride in the world they had just conquered in Christ's name. Lope's plays reflected his age's secular preoccupations: the spirit of intrigue, heroic action, and all the frivolities of the grand spectacle blended with popular slapstick. Calderón clothed the world in the Spanish black cape of honor, religious fatality, and the vivid promise of release from this weary earth into heaven. The people loved Calderón passionately and trembled before the austere lyricism of his plays. But in Lope they rejoiced, for his was mostly the anarchic spirit. His best poetry always flowed from an active consciousness of communion with a popular audience. Before Lope's spectacle, the heart raced and danced to the flip of jaunty street phrases and peasant aphorisms, and to the music of the ballad known to each Spaniard from the cradle. With Calderón, the heart stood still, chilled by the spectacle of divine mercy and the saints' misericordia, aching for an escape beyond the blind lusts of mortality.

Lorca discovered a solid base for his poetic drama precisely in Lope and Calderón. Like Lope, he is essentially a lyric poet whose dramatic instinct grew out of a sense of communication he felt himself able to establish with the people. He too was possessed with the need to create spectacle, a visual and musical supplement to the art of the spoken word. Lorca's work also has a close moral affinity with Calderón's drama. Like Calderón, he seems to reduce life to a symbolic formula, holds that traditional Spanish respect for honor, and sees on life's flashing mosaic face the essential mask of death. But if on these terms Lorca's drama lacks the old unity, it is because he could not find grace, as Calderón did, in heaven, or absolution from the sins of human perversity on earth, the Catholic Church notwithstanding. He had no answer to the questions which most obsessed him. But he was fired with the fine musical imagination of a minstrel, and the sharp sense of death magnified—magnified as a garden in the clear morning light, to the least inconsiderable weed. With the first he wove out his dramatic idea; with the second he set his scene; and with both he opened the eyes of an audience which had not been stirred by such display for over two centuries.

Growing out of his consistent innovations in the lyric medium, Lorca's development as a dramatist fulfilled the imaginative pattern of his whole art. He was branching out only because his roots were still energetically producing new and firmer fruit from the store of his original obsessions. With few other modern writers is it possible to point to such a sure and healthy growth. With fewer still is it possible to speak of the same sincerity of artistic purpose. More specifically, a striking analogy suggests itself between Lorca's dramatic intentions and those of the guiding spirits of the Irish National movement in literature at the beginning of this century.

In his preface to *The Playboy of the Western World,* John Millington Synge wrote:

> On the stage one must have reality, and one must have joy; and that is why the intellectual modern drama has failed, and people have grown sick of the false joy of the musical comedy, that has been given them in place of the rich joy found only in what is superb and wild in reality. In a good play every speech should be as fully flavored as a nut or apple, and such speeches cannot be written by anyone who works among people who have shut their lips on poetry.

The positive dramatic thing which Synge was seeking and trying himself to do in the theatre was also the business of García Lorca. For, like Synge and Yeats and Lady Gregory when they set out to create a national literature for the Irish theatre, Lorca was rebelling against the realistic middle-class drama, which in Spain had succeeded in shutting off from the stage the rich atmosphere of folk speech and imagination. Lorca tried to break through the commercialized theatre with its vulgar parades of life twisted into the neat cynical gesture, the always triumphant negative morality. What he, like those leaders of the Irish movement, proposed to put in its place was the sense of the magic of language to which only a people still attached to the rituals of the land could respond with authentic pleasure. In Ireland, however, with Synge's premature death and Yeats' disdain for the howling theatre mobs which turned him into a writer for the very few, the inspired movement lost much of its vitality. But when death interrupted Lorca, he had already passed further

**110**

into the world of folk drama than either Synge or Yeats. For he not only gave the stage a "rich joy," but re-established the tragedy of the folk by a poetic vision which touches on the whole modern situation as well.

Lorca's earliest dramatic attempt, *El Maleficio de la Mariposa* (*The Witchery of the Butterfly*), is a short poetic fantasy. It concerns the thwarted idealism of a humble cockroach who has been given a sudden insight into another world by accidental contact with a wounded butterfly. This play—or rather, this fragile dramatic poem —written before the author was twenty and in the first months of his residence in Madrid, was staged during the 1919–20 theatrical season by Martínez Sierra. Since it was never published,[1] few facts regarding it are known. Fortunately, however, the Argentine writer, Alfredo de la Guardia, who has written extensively on Lorca's art, witnessed the only performance of the play, and is in a position to describe it in some detail. De la Guardia's record is valuable because it makes clear those elements in the play which suggest Lorca's whole future development as poet and dramatist. The plot may be summarized briefly:

On a fine summer day, a brilliantly colored butterfly suddenly falls into the tall grass of an Andalusian field, among a startled colony of cockroaches. Life for these lowly insects is momentarily interrupted. Gossip runs high among them, since they have never seen a butterfly before. There is speculation, especially among the older cockroaches, about the meaning of this visitation. Is this dazzling creature, whose wing has been wounded in its giddy passage through air and clouds, a good angel or a ma-

[1] A manuscript of this play, missing the last few pages, was discovered and appears in *Obras Completas* (Aguilar, 1960).

111

levolent enchantress? Although the butterfly is hospitably received by all, cautious parents warn their offspring to stay away from the mysterious intruder. But there is one cockroach who will not heed these warnings. Hypnotized by her beauty and throbbing with curiosity, he emerges from the dark earth to approach her. Fearful at first of the light and color she sheds over all, he gradually grows bold enough to engage her in conversation. He asks about her world of sunlight and flowers and blue sky. What she tells him agitates him so with longing that he secretly tests his own short, black wings for flight. But he cannot rise above the grass. Finally, the day comes when the enchantress, regaining the use of her wings, flies away into the light before the anguished eyes of the cockroach. She disappears from sight, while he muses over the open-air paradise she has described to him—the world he will never know. Now he is completely disoriented. He can no longer breathe in the dark earth while her bright vision is reflected in his eyes. His life now and forever will be tormented by "the witchery of the butterfly."

Except for the lively applause of a few friends scattered in the audience, *El Maleficio de la Mariposa* was vociferously booed by those who saw its only performance. Indeed there must have been little in it for an audience used to the dexterous middle-class comedies of the Quintero brothers, the rhetorical poetic plays of the indefatigable Eduardo Marquina, and the talkative moral dramas of Jacinto Benavente. The Madrid audience was out for its customary "slice of life," and was naturally outraged by the febrile imaginings of a boy poet. If there was nothing strikingly original about Lorca's first dramatic work, it

**112**

does indicate that his initial approach to drama was through the poetic imagination, which was gradually to invade the whole of his work in the theatre. The subject he had chosen, like all those he chose later for his plays, was immanent, if not already developed, in his verse. One of his earliest poems, "Los Encuentros de un Caracol Aventurero" ("The Encounters of an Adventurous Snail"), had hinted at the theme of *El Maleficio de la Mariposa*. The poem describes the "pacific, ignorant and humble" snail, "bourgeois of the path," who ventures into the brush, stirred by a quixotic feeling to see "the end of the road." He encounters among other things a colony of ants beating one of their number to death. He interrupts to question them, and the dying victim explains that he is receiving punishment for having seen the stars. Never having seen the stars himself, the snail asks what they are like. The beaten ant replies they are "lights which we carry over our heads." The other ants have never seen them either; they have been too busy working. But the offender, having mounted to the topmost part of a tree, had seen them from there. He is perverse and lazy, and since "to work is the law," the ants have decided he must die. At the last moment, the dying ant sees a bee hovering above him in the soft air, and expires with the words, "She has come to carry me off to a star." "Full of confusion for the eternal," the snail concludes that it is suicidal to think of the stars and of the road's end.

The verses of this fable are pedestrian; but the design of tragedy is already sketched within them: hunger for the illimitable; a society whose moral laws are severe unto death; the suffering which comes of frustration; and the

**113**

inevitable punishment meted out to the innocent of spirit. Beyond this, but implicit in both poem and dramatic fantasy, is the lure of Andalusia, the open-air paradise pulsing with love and death.

Of Lorca's second work for the theatre, *Títeres de Cachiporra: La Niña Que Riega la Albahaca y el Príncipe Preguntón* (*Puppet Show: The Girl Who Waters the Sweet Basil Flower and the Inquisitive Prince*), little more than the title is established. Written for a celebration of the Twelfth-Night holiday, it was presented to a small group of friends in Granada, with Manuel de Falla at the piano. Another significant puppet show, *Retablillo de Don Cristóbal* (*In the Frame of Don Cristóbal*), which was written and produced several years later, finally found its way into print.

Lorca's first full-length play, *Mariana Pineda,* appeared before a Madrid audience in the autumn of 1927. Perhaps with more reason than modesty, Lorca chose the subtitle "Romance Popular en Tres Estampas" ("Popular Ballad in Three Prints"). Although he makes good use of certain limited stage techniques, the play's unity is centered in the poetic treatment of the idea, suffused by an antique nineteenth century atmosphere and set in "three prints." It is important to state again that the author is not merely trying to put something wholly frivolous on the stage; any good dramatist knows how precarious it is to sacrifice movement and gesture for poetic language in the modern theatre. In being poetic, Lorca's attempt in the tragic form was necessarily experimental; yet, in many ways, his future integrity as a dramatic writer depended on its success.

*Mariana Pineda* has few pretensions, therefore, to being

a drama in the conventional sense, with fully articulated tragic consequences. For one thing, little effort is spent on the individualization of characters. For another, the resolution is not implicit in the action of the play so much as in a mystic idea which takes refuge with the heroine. And finally, it is through the development of this idea that one comes upon the proper instigator of dramatic emotion, Granada itself; so that above all human involvements, the spirit guiding the whole action is really the Granadine circumambience. Of all solutions to the dramatic and moral complications of frustrated love, Lorca arrives at the most distinctly impersonal one. Through certain anonymous demands made by the Granadine surroundings, the character of Mariana is impelled towards acts and feelings which, thus becoming typical and irrevocable, transcend the private tragedy. The mode of presentation is intentionally romantic, heroic, stylized; the method is spectacular, lyric, and episodic. The result is the transposition of a personal problem into the anonymity of history.

Mariana Pineda, the widowed mother of two children, figured as the Betsy Ross in the early nineteenth century liberal movement in Spain. A native of Granada, she sewed the flag of liberty for the republican conspirators who were trying to overthrow the monarchy of Ferdinand VII. Caught by the king's police, she was found guilty of treason and hanged. These are the bare facts. Without altering the actual events, Lorca recasts Mariana Pineda into a symbol of human freedom, draped from head to foot in the spirit of Granada. She is portrayed as a woman whose love is instinct with so much of the human that it reaches out to the divine. She can only give, from what she is and has, but cannot take, because satisfaction in earthly love has been denied her. Accepting the martyrdom which is her fate, she is born to suffer and die so that others may better understand how to live, though none imitate her. With this consciousness, Lorca touches the Spanish national pride in its martyrs, and while personalizing history, he seeks to uncover the moral idea which is the source of all myths. The yellow "print" in which each of the three scenes is framed gives the effect of a commemorative representation suddenly coming to life through the use of a recurring ballad motif. This effect becomes an immediate transfer of mood which restores to the stage the living past of a particular moment in history.

Before the curtain rises on the first "print," a group of young girls sing two stanzas from a century-old children's song describing Mariana's tragedy:

> ¡Oh! Qué día tan triste en Granada,
> que a las piedras hacía llorar
> al ver que Marianita se muere
> en cadalso por no declarar.
>
> Marianita, sentada en su cuarto,
> no paraba de considerar:
> "Si Pedrosa me viera bordando
> la bandera de la Libertad."

> (Oh, that day in Granada so full of distress
> that even the stones had to cry
> seeing Marianita die
> on the gallows for refusing to confess.
>
> Sitting in her room, Marianita
> did not stop to consider:

116

"What if Pedrosa should see me
sewing the banner of Liberty?")

Then the play immediately opens upon a view of Mariana's
home in Granada. The air is yellow with light, and blue
with shadow, the room full of quinces and roses: a domestic setting which forms the quiet backdrop to Mariana's
growing anxiety. Doña Angustias, her foster mother, and
Clavela, a maid, discuss Mariana's strange activity: her
sewing a flag for the liberals. Clavela can only think her be-
witched, while Doña Angustias suggests more accurately
that she is in love. Two frivolous girls of the neighborhood
appear, and their attempt to entertain Mariana with their
chatter and a picturesque ballad about the bull-ring at
Ronda only saddens the woman, who is awaiting a more
important visitation. Later, an admiring adolescent comes
to see her, and in the midst of their discussion, a mysterious
rider arrives with a message from her lover, the escaped
leader of the liberal forces, Don Pedro Sotomayor. She
anxiously dispatches her young admirer to bring Don Pedro from the mountains where he is hiding.

Throughout the first "print," Mariana is confused and
fearful. She is conscious of her anomalous position, the
threat to her respectability of her recent action, and the
growing suspicion of the king's constable, Pedrosa. From
this outer perplexity we see her retreating into the inner
world of her convictions where she has identified her love
for Don Pedro Sotomayor with his love for liberty. There
is an instability in her love which the mournful echoes of
Granada's streets seem to emphasize. We have reason to
believe that her love will take on a mystical form as her
passion increases.

**117**

The second "print" reopens on the domestic vignette. Clavela is preparing Mariana's two children for bed, when they insist she sing the ballad of the girl who sewed the banner for the Duke of Lucén. This is a striking, intentional miniature, a print within a print, suggesting the alter-ego of Mariana Pineda herself, especially in the verses, "The flag which I am sewing will come to no avail." When the children are put to bed, Don Pedro appears. The scene becomes ephemeral with the feeling that though the lovers embrace they do not belong to each other. A contrary dream stands between. Pedro speaks in flat impassioned abstractions that do not readily convince.

The rest of the conspirators arrive: a weary, incredibly timorous lot. Pedro explains to them how inevitable it is that all Andalusia, so naturally endowed with spiritual freedom and alive to his vision, should declare itself politically free from the king. But there is a little mote of fanatical blindness in his eye, which Mariana's practical sense discovers without being able to remove. A messenger arrives to report the failure of the revolutionary movement in Cádiz, and the betrayal of Torrijos, the liberal general there. The event, presented in ballad form, seems to free itself from the poet's hand and fall into the anonymity of folk feeling, its perfected expression.

When they learn that the king's constable is on his way, the conspirators cheer themselves with the sound of their own voices. Here, the only affirmative thing about Pedro is his decision to leave Mariana behind. And she is left to face Pedrosa, the constable, alone. Fierce, dry, old, and inquisitorial, he readily penetrates her secret, revealing his knowledge of her complicity in the plot. He goes after her hungrily, but encounters Mariana's ardent insistence on her womanly honor. When Pedrosa leaves, giving official notice of her arrest, Mariana momentarily runs to escape the way of the conspirators. But it is not her way, for she has herself created her doom. Outwardly, she is recalled by the sound of her crying children.

The third "print," withdrawing from the hectic action of the second, is concerned solely with defining Mariana's spirit. It is a quiet Arabic setting, in the Convent of Santa María Egipcíaca, amid the distant murmurs of an organ and nuns' voices. Here all is sympathy for her. The lines of a saint have been etched in her suffering, as indeed an actual halo is described about her head by the two little novices discussing her tragedy. Moreover, Mariana herself has slowly slipped into the role:

> Soy una gran pecadora;
> pero amé de una manera
> que Dios me perdonará
> como a Santa Magdalena.

> (I am a great sinner,
> but I loved in such a way
> that God will pardon me
> as He did Saint Magdalene.)

She soons learns that Don Pedro and the conspirators have escaped safely to England. But she scoffs at the idea; her illusion, having lived for so long within her, is still credible enough to warm her hopes. All the same, there is an inner voice which tells her—it is described as a gypsy voice out of Granada—"by the edge of the water/ without a soul's seeing it,/ my hope was drowned."

**119**

When Pedrosa comes to offer her freedom if she will divulge the names of the conspirators, Mariana is already beyond worldly appeal; she has begun to enact the conviction in her own martyrdom. Conscious as a dream made real, she is the living symbol of love and agony. But, of course, Pedro had really only little to do with what she has become; it was her own created passion, the flame of her life, her revelation as a woman. Her last words before she is led away to the executioner are entirely the words of a conscious martyr, whose vision has magnified her personal cry till it reaches toward something universal:

> *Amas la Libertad por encima de todo,*
> *pero yo soy la misma Libertad. Doy mi sangre,*
> *que es tu sangre y la sangre de todas las criaturas.*
> *¡No se podrá comprar el corazón de nadie!*
> *Ahora sí lo que dicen el ruiseñor y el árbol.*
> *El hombre es un cautivo y no puede librarse.*
>
> .  .  .  .  .  .  .
>
> *¡Yo soy la Libertad herida por los hombres!*
> *¡Amor, amor, amor y eternas soledades!*

> (Above everything, you love Liberty.
> But I am Liberty itself. I give my blood
> which is your blood and the blood of all living things.
> Nobody's heart can be bought!
> Now the nightingale and the tree say so.
> Man is a captive and cannot liberate himself.
>
> .  .  .  .  .  .  .
>
> I am Liberty wounded by men!
> Love, love, love and eternal solitude!)

And so Mariana dies in the name of Liberty. If she had died only for her lover as one man, or if she had merely lived on in torment, her life's meaning would have been obscured, a story of humiliation. Incapable of the mystic sacrifice, she would have had only her stiff bewilderment to contemplate and the doughy look of a frightened lover to haunt her days. It is a pagan support—the warm, re-signed cry of Granada—however, which rescues Mariana from such indecencies and which, paradoxically enough, makes her tragedy a Christian one.

This adaptation of historical material is particularly fortunate for Lorca's purposes. It establishes a frame of reference, in the habit of Greek drama, which not only assures the audience's immediate response, but also limits the activity of the poet's inventions within an always communicable reality. Furthermore, it affords the constant possibility of a new and original emphasis which the poet is trying to create according to his own preoccupations. The only danger threatening the unity of conception is one which is responsible for the essential flaw in *Mariana Pineda:* the lack of proportion between the historical facts themselves and the re-creation of character credible enough to enact them.

If it is assumed, in dramatic terms, that the action of heroism, which is Mariana's sacrifice in the cause of Liberty, is a conscious thing of which only a person confident of her action is capable, then Mariana comes close to being unconvincing. The sudden transition of her love from the man to his cause, which he holds dearer than herself, blots out the meaning of love itself. From the beginning we are confronted with Mariana's heroism as a compensation for an unrealized love, and therefore, a love which was never well established. We must believe that the impulse leading

121

to Mariana's final action had nothing at all to do with the zeal of a political or religious idealist, or with the transformation which a passionate love might stimulate, but that it had everything to do with some mystic summons of the Granadine environment. The only means of understanding Mariana completely is through the spirit of Granada which Lorca tries continually to communicate through her in the play. To say he has not succeeded in doing this would be to criticize him for what no artist could fairly be expected to do within one short work. It must rather be said that what he succeeded in communicating of Granada is not sufficient to support Mariana feasibly as a woman. We can only accept her visionary experience as a fact beside the historic one, which is somewhere between the poetic representation and the religious passion. In other words, the emotional experience *Mariana Pineda* summons up is something which resembles the experience one is likely to have listening to a sonata. To a varying degree this holds true for most of Lorca's plays; they cannot be viewed simply within the category of conventional drama. For too often do they gain completeness only in the musical imagination. And for an ordinary audience, this readjustment is quite difficult to make.

The reception given *Mariana Pineda,* though favorable, still did not suggest that alacrity of response which the writer was seeking in his audience. Perhaps it was because they had been for so long unused to poetry of this kind on the stage, or because they found no comfort in the story, which was itself slight and nothing remarkable. But Lorca was convinced that this sluggishness was due more to imaginative sloth, and that his audience had to be re-educated to "see life" in the theatre. This conviction becomes plain in the group of productions which followed *Mariana Pineda*.

The first is a series of three farces written between 1927 and 1931: *Amor de Don Perlimplín con Belisa en Su Jardín* (*Love of Don Perlimplín for Belisa in His Garden*); *La Zapatera Prodigiosa* (*The Shoemaker's Wonderful Wife*); and *Retablillo de Don Cristóbal* (*In the Frame of Don Cristóbal*). Though comprising a minor part of Lorca's output, each of these works reaffirms the poet's propriety in the theatre. The first, most striking in technical ingenuity and scenic originality, continues the idea of a period "print" enacted in a theatrical frame. The atmosphere of the sensual young Belisa pervades the idiom, the stage décor, the costumes, the music of the whole piece, till one perceives that it bursts from a single imagination endowed with the same richness in all its facets.

Perlimplín, a well-to-do, retiring, and bookish bachelor of fifty, is urged by his housekeeper, Marcolfa, to marry the seductive Belisa who lives next door. In eighteenth century fashion, he is dressed in a green cassock and wears a white wig full of curls. He is childishly horrified at the thought of marriage, and is reminded of a shoemaker's young wife who strangled her elderly husband. But yielding to his housekeeper, Perlimplín timidly asks Belisa's hand of her mother—a lady quick to see the profitable nature of the match—who in turn accedes with surprising and comic readiness. Belisa, a fertile unselfconscious body of earth yearning to find a lover, is revealed half-naked in her balcony window across from Perlimplín, singing:

> Amor, amor.
> Entre mis muslos cerrados,
> nada como un pez el sol.
> Agua tibia entre los juncos,
> amor.
> ¡Gallo que se va la noche!
> ¡Que no se vaya, no!

> (Love, love.
> Enclosed by my thighs,
> the sun swims like a fish.
> Warm water among the rushes,
> love.
> Cock, the night is going!
> Don't let it go, no!)

A fluttering of paper birds in the window ends this scene, the play's prologue.

In the first scene of the "only act," a huge bed is displayed in Perlimplín's room, radiating the voluptuousness of the wedding night with its colors and down comforters, its canopy of plumes and soft cushions. Six doors lead into the room, and the whole is described as slightly wrong in perspective, like a carelessly placed wall-hanging. Perlimplín, attired in lace ruffs and furs, sedately bids Marcolfa leave. Belisa, thinly dressed in her sleeping gown, hair loose and arms bare, walks to the bed and lies down. Guitars are heard in the distance. Perlimplín trembles with fear and the knowledge of his own age before a desire he feels incapable of consummating. Belisa is frank and warm. He throws a red cape over her. Five whistles are heard. Perlimplín suspects intruders, but Belisa tells him languorously that it is only the clock. When he goes to bed, two sprites enter and run a misty curtain across the stage. Seated on the prompter's box, they face the audience, discuss the secrets being unfolded behind the curtain, and half-mock the audience for its curiosity:

Don't leave a cranny open, for the crannies of today are the obscurities of tomorrow. When things are quite apparent, Man thinks there's no need to look further into them and he goes to obscure things to discover the secrets he already knows.

When they leave, blue hoods over their heads, they open the curtain on Perlimplín, seated fully dressed in bed with two horns grown out of his forehead, gilded and beflowered. The five balconies to the room are open with the white light of dawn piercing through each. Perlimplín inspects them and discovers five ladders hung to the ground and five hats beneath them. Belisa blithely informs him that they are evidence of the "little drunkards who come and go." Paper birds flutter across the windows again as Perlimplín, sitting at the bedside, watches Belisa fall asleep and proclaims his undying love.

The second scene opens on Perlimplín's dining room, which is again arranged so that the perspective is "deliciously wrong." Objects on the table are painted as for the Last Supper. In tears, Marcolfa explains that those who entered her master's bedroom on his wedding night were representatives of the five races on earth: the European, the Indian, the Negro, the Yellow, and the American. She hints that Belisa has already been seeing a young man. At this, Belisa herself enters wearing a voluminous red dress in eighteenth century fashion, with the skirt slit in the back, allowing the whole length of her stockinged leg to be seen. Her earrings are tremendous and her red hat is adorned with ostrich feathers. She enters thinking aloud of her lover, whom she has not seen but whose imminent appearance makes her "breasts tremble." Perlimplín enters just when a note wrapped about a stone is hurled onto the balcony. He takes it up jokingly despite her pleas to surrender it. Returning it then, he says he has been noticing things and feels hurt, but that he understands she is living in a drama. She comforts him with vows of her faithfulness. But Perlimplín declares he has learned her secret and wants to help her. He admits knowing the young man, whose beauty, he assures her, is dazzling. Perlimplín will love her as a father only. Belisa is pleased by this new turn and speaks frankly of her new love's curiosity. She has been receiving letters very different from those of former lovers who spoke only of dreams and far-off lands. The mysterious new lover writes simply of her soft body. Perlimplín points to a figure in the garden, and when Belisa looks, it is gone. Perlimplín leaves, telling her she is "beyond the morals of the world," and promising a new development.

In the third and final scene, Perlimplín is whispering with his housekeeper in the garden. Marcolfa weeps because her respectable master has allowed himself to play cuckold. With bravado, Perlimplín states that it is so because he has no honor. Marcolfa, shocked by this heresy, is anxious to leave the household at once. Perlimplín urges her to stay and to help carry out his little plan. Then he hides behind some rosebushes as Belisa enters singing. A serenade is being played in the moonlight when the figure of a young man, with a red cape thrown over him, appears from the bushes and darts across the lawn. Recognizing him, Belisa calls and receives a sign that he will return later. She is immersed in an erotically dreamy passion when Perlimplín enters. She tells him that the perfume she senses from her lover's body has fired her love. Perlimplín answers that such is his triumph, "the triumph of my imagination." Belisa admits, "It's true that you helped me love him." And Perlimplín adds, "As I shall now help you mourn him." The clock strikes ten.

PERLIMPLÍN: The hour has come!
BELISA: He should be here in a few moments.
PERLIMPLÍN: He's leaping the walls of my garden.
BELISA: Wrapped in his red cape.
PERLIMPLÍN (*drawing a dagger*): Red as his blood.

Belisa tries to restrain him; Perlimplín embraces her and asks if she loves the young man. When she affirms this, he explains:

In view of the fact that you love him so much, I don't want him to abandon you. And so that he may be yours completely, it has occurred to me that the best thing is to stick this dagger into his gallant heart. . . . Thus, when he is dead, you will be able to caress him eternally in your bed, so handsome and spruced up, without fearing that he will stop loving you. He will love you with the infinite love of the dead, and I'll be free of this dark nightmare of your sumptuous body . . . Your body! . . . whose meaning I should never be able to decipher.

Perlimplín runs after a form that has disappeared into the bushes. Belisa, almost hysterical with love and torment,

**127**

begs for a sword to slit her husband's throat. Wrapped in a red cape, a wounded man comes stumbling through the bushes. Belisa embraces the figure, removes the cape and discovers Perlimplín, who tells her he has been killed by her husband with an emerald dagger, now sticking out of his chest:

When he wounded me, he shouted, 'Now Belisa has a soul!' . . . Perlimplín killed me. . . . Ah, Don Perlimplín, youthful old man, puppet without strength, you couldn't enjoy Belisa's body. . . . Belisa's body was intended for younger muscles and lips of burning coal. . . . While I loved your body and nothing more . . . your body!

Belisa hugs him without quite realizing the deception. When Perlimplín falls dead in her arms, she is still asking, "But the young man?" Marcolfa, who has been an accomplice in the act, enters sorrowfully to find Belisa weeping over Perlimplín's body.

BELISA (*weeping*): I never believed he was so complicated.

MARCOLFA: You awake to it too late. I will make a crown of flowers like the midday sun.

BELISA (*removed, as if in another world*): Perlimplín, what have you done, Perlimplín?

Marcolfa says that now Belisa is another woman, "dressed in the most glorious blood of my master." "But who was this man?" Belisa asks.

MARCOLFA: The beautiful adolescent whose face you'll never see.

BELISA: Yes, yes, Marcolfa, I love him, I love him with all the strength of my body and soul. But where is the young man in the red cape? My God, where is he?

MARCOLFA: Don Perlimplín, sleep in peace. . . . Do you hear her? Don Perlimplín. . . . Do you hear her?

**128**

And so, through his suicide, the tragi-comedian has achieved the triumph of his imagination: he has given the warm Belisa a soul.

Though less ambitious than his later tragedies, *Don Perlimplín* shows Lorca at his best in fusing the imaginative conviction of his poetry with the dramatic devices of the farce. Had he lived longer, it is entirely possible that such efforts might have carried him further in the poetic drama than any writer of his time. The kind of dramatic inventiveness he displays in *Don Perlimplín* and later in *Así Que Pasen Cinco Años* brings to the theatre that subtle interplay between farce and tragedy which the best expressionist drama of our time has often lacked.

In the second of this series, *La Zapatera Prodigiosa* (*The Shoemaker's Wonderful Wife*), Lorca wrote a pure Andalusian folk comedy in the tradition of Alarcón's *El Sombrero de Tres Picos* (*The Three-Cornered Hat*). The author himself mounts the stage to create the intimacy he desires with the audience, and to explain to them, half playfully, half seriously, exactly what they may not hope to expect from him:

My worthy audience . . . (*Pause*) No, not "worthy audience"; simply "audience." And not because the author does not consider his audience worthy—quite the contrary. But behind that word there is a delicate tremor of fear and a kind of plea that the audience be generous with the players' efforts and the author's contrivances. The poet does not ask for benevolence, but for attention—since he has long ago leaped over that dangerous hurdle of fear which authors have for the theatre. Because of this absurd fear and because the theatre is often simply a commercial enterprise, poetry retires from the stage looking for other surroundings where people will not be surprised that a tree, for example, should become a puff of smoke or that three fishes, for love of a hand or a word, should become three million fishes to satisfy the hunger of a multitude. The author has preferred to set forth his dramatic example in the lively rhythm of a familiar little shoemaker's wife. Everywhere there breathes just such a poetic being whom the author has dressed as a shoemaker's wife with a single ballad or the refrain of a song. Let the audience not think it strange, therefore, if she appears violent or if she assumes bitter postures, because she is always fighting, fighting with the reality surrounding her and fighting with fantasy when it turns into visible reality. (*Shouts of the Shoemaker's Wife are heard:* I want to come on!) I'm going! Don't be so impatient to come on. You're not wearing a gown with a long train and fantastic feathers, but a tattered little dress. Do you hear? The dress of a shoemaker's wife. (*Voice of the Shoemaker's Wife inside:* I want to come on!) Silence! (*The curtain is drawn and the stage is seen in soft light.*) Every day it dawns like this in the cities, and people forget their half-world of dreams to go into the markets, just as you in your house on the stage, my wonderful little shoemaker's wife. (*The light is growing brighter.*) To begin with: you come into the street. (*Quarrelsome voices are heard. Author to the audience:*) Good night. (*He lifts his hat by the crown and as he does so a green light is seen shining within. The author tips his hat and a stream of water falls over him. The author glances about at his audience with some restraint and draws backward, leaving with profound irony.*) I beg your pardon. (*Exit.*)

It may be noted that Lorca's emphasis here is poetic rather than dramatic; that he mocks the devices of the conventional drama, insisting instead on the place of fantasy and imagination in the theatre, which will be a miracle to the eyes and spirit—as the miracle of Christ and the three fishes; and finally, that the greatest miracles are those accomplished without artifice in the daily run of life. What follows is a performance which lives up to the spirit of the introduction. A thin plot notwithstanding, the poetry,

**130**

song, spectacle and rich folk speech merge into one gay quick movement of dramatic inevitability. Lorca struggled hard during the next few years to bring the same simplicity of mood to shape his folk tragedies.

There is some evidence in the theme of this comedy, innocent and joyful as it seems in its depiction of a peasant girl's happy resolution of her marital problem, which points to the pathos in his later folk tragedies. Conscious of her beauty and youth, the Shoemaker's Wife feels irrevocably tied down to her seemingly tired, conscientious and colorless old husband. (An echo, it will be remembered, of Don Perlimplín's first fear of marriage and its possible consequences, as based on the sordid story of a shoemaker's wife who strangled her husband.) Ultimately, her flirtations and tempestuous outbursts drive a patient husband out into the world; then she is compelled to deal with the gossip of the neighbors and the scandals which have been evoked by her turning the bootshop into a tavern where suitors come to drink and make advances. Though she keeps her precious honor intact, she is almost led to distraction by the suspicions of the neighborhood. Only in the end, when she is reunited to her husband (who, disguised as a traveling puppet-master, returns to prove her constancy), does she triumph over the moral outrage of her neighbors. But even so, one feels this is probably not enough to regain her position in society, or even perhaps, to quiet her hidden sense of betrayal in marriage.

Could it have been that what Lorca was seeking most in this period was a sense of freedom with his material, using the popular vein of comedy as a source from which to embark on more daring flights? This seems confirmed in

**131**

the third of these works, the puppet farce *Retablillo de Don Cristóbal* (*In the Frame of Don Cristóbal*). Born as pure folk banter and free of the poet's later complex contrivances, this little dramatic piece has the quick momentum of a kind of logical action peculiar to itself—a quality which his better and more serious work sometimes misses. Even the intrusion of the poet as a character, his public altercation with and humility before the director, is completely justified by the ingenuous spirit of the farce. What is said about the play and what the play itself says are not two things, but one. The poet is made part of his own dream's expression in a way which no other dramatic form would allow. This sudden joy of identification is struck in the opening:

## PROLOGUE

Ladies and Gentlemen:

The poet who has interpreted and adapted this puppet farce from the lips of the people has evidence of the fact that the distinguished audience this afternoon will be able to appreciate intelligently and good-heartedly the deliciously crude language of the puppets.

Every popular puppet show has the same rhythm, the same fantasy, and the same enchanting sense of freedom which the poet has here conserved in the dialogue.

The puppet show is the expression of the people's imagination, giving the temperature of its grace and its innocence.

The poet knows that the audience will hear with joy and simplicity the expressions born from the earth; and that these will serve as purifiers now, when vulgarities, falsehoods, and strained feelings reach deepest into the home.

(*Enter, the* POET)

POET: Men and women, attention! Child, be still! I want you to

**132**

be so quiet, so profoundly still, that we shall be able to hear the glu-glu of the fountains. And if a bird should shake its wing, let us also hear it; and if a little ant should move its foot, let us also hear it; and if a heart should beat loudly, let it seem like a hand dividing the rushes at the shore. Oh, no! It will be necessary for the young ladies to close their fans and for the girls to take off their silken kerchiefs, so that we may hear and see all this business about Rosita, married to Cristóbal, and all this business about Cristóbal, married to Rosita.

My! They are beating the drum. You may weep or you may laugh. It doesn't matter to me in the least what you do. I'm going to eat a little bread now, the tiniest bit of bread which the birds have left me; and then I'm going to press the costumes of the company. (*Looks around to see if he is being observed.*) I want to tell you that I know how roses are born and how the stars grew out of the sea, but. . . .

DIRECTOR: Please favor us with keeping still! The Prologue ends where you say, "I'm going to press the costumes of the company."

POET: Yes, sir.

DIRECTOR: As a poet you have no business prying into the secrets in which we all live.

POET: Yes, sir.

DIRECTOR: Don't I pay you a decent salary?

POET: Yes, sir; but I want to say that I know that at heart Cristóbal is good, and perhaps could be so.

DIRECTOR: Loud mouth! If you don't shut up, I'll break your crust of corn bread in half. Who are you to determine the laws of good and evil?

POET: I'm finished; I'll be still.

DIRECTOR: No, sir! Say what you are expected to say, and what the audience knows to be true.

POET: Honorable people: As a poet I am obliged to inform you that Cristóbal is bad.

DIRECTOR: And he cannot be good.

POET: And he cannot be good.

DIRECTOR: All right, let's go now.

POET: I'm coming, Mr. Director. And he never can be any good.

DIRECTOR: Very well. Now, how much do I owe you?

POET: Five coins.

DIRECTOR: Here you are.

POET: No! I don't want it in gold. Gold is like fire, and I am a poet of the night. Give it to me in silver. Silver coins will be lit up by the moon.

DIRECTOR: Ha, ha! So much the better for me. Now to begin.

And so we are introduced to Cristóbal, who buys the erotic creature Rosita in marriage with a promise to her mother, temperamentally as greedy and frightened as a procuress. (Again, this recalls the opening scene of *Don Perlimplín.*) But the marriage comes to no good, since Rosita deceives her husband while he lies asleep by giving herself to all the male characters, including the Poet and the Invalid, whom Cristóbal robbed and beat to death in order to marry her. When, a moment later, Rosita gives birth to quadruplets, Cristóbal wakes and maliciously takes his vengeance by beating the Mother to death when she insists that they are his children; she can even raise her head posthumously and shout, "Yours! Yours!" to his still furious questioning.

In this very period when he was vivifying the folk idiom on his stage, Lorca was also writing another series of plays, adaptations in the remote and highly involved style of surrealism. These plays were never produced, and information concerning them is still incomplete. During the years 1929–1930, he wrote *Así Que Pasen Cinco Años* (*When Five Years Pass*) and *El Público* (*The Audience*). (This is the same period of his restless quest for a new imagery, already outlined in his New York poems. And Lorca's friends suggest the existence of several stories and prose

**134**

poems done in the same manner. Among these, *Suicidio en Alejandría* [*Suicide in Alexandria*] and *La Gallina* [*The Hen*] are mentioned.[1]) The unrevised but complete manuscript of *Así Que Pasen Cinco Años* was subsequently published among his *Obras Completas;* but only two scenes of the full drama, *El Público*, have yet appeared. There is evidence of something exciting and new in content, but at the same time a sense of confusion in dramatic focus, which may be due both to the tentative manner of Lorca's approach and to the inconclusive state in which we find the works. Unresolved or fragmentary, they are nevertheless important experiments in the use of musical structure as a basis for dramatic operation.

*Así Que Pasen Cinco Años,* published with the subtitle, "A Legend of the Times in Three Acts and Five Scenes," is the longest and most difficult of Lorca's plays. Its unrealized possibilities become evident as the poet's brusque inventiveness outspeeds the progress of the slight dramatic theme, as characters slip in and fade out for undisclosed reasons, and the nature of the inanimate and the animal becomes more profound than the human. If one remembers how eagerly Lorca sought freedom for his imagination in the theatre, how he attempted to break down the barrier between stage and audience, it is possible to see why surrealistic devices should have interested him. Certainly there has never been anything in the theatre which one might call a surrealist *form*. Lorca's experiment in this direction, however, was not particularly original. Maeterlinck, Pirandello, O'Neill, Strindberg, and Čapek had used, with both marked and indifferent success, certain new imaginative formulas on the stage, by which critics

[1] These now appear in *Obras Completas* (Aguilar, 1960).

learned to argue new terms— Expressionism, Symbolism, Constructivism, etc. Quite as daring were the attempts of Azorín, Gómez de la Serna, Alberti, Cocteau, Breton, and a host of lesser surrealists who combined earlier technical innovations with their own fanciful projections, striving for a more startling "reality" or "super-reality" on a transformed stage. If much of this work did go to waste because of obscurantism and the dramatist's flaunting contempt for his audience, the product was not always without genuine esthetic value. And even if Lorca should finally have found this procedure the wrong instrument for his purpose in the theatre, there is no doubt that through it he became for the first time creatively conscious of his dramatic limitations.

As in most Expressionistic drama, the characters of *Así Que Pasen Cinco Años* have no proper names; they are merely the Young Man, the Old Man, the Stenographer, the Friends, the Child, the Betrothed, the Football Player, the Manikin, etc. In the first act, the Young Man is conversing in his library with the Old Man. The former is committed to waiting five years for the return of his Betrothed, and is wholly lost in memories which seem more real to him than the actuality of love. The Old Man agrees with him in this, but adds significantly that the important thing is "to remember beforehand . . . toward tomorrow." A clock strikes six when the Stenographer silently crosses the stage. They continue discussing the Young Man's Betrothed, and the sedentary tragedy of his life is revealed. He feels enclosed by four walls, yet he cannot stand the noises, heat and bad odors of the street. The Valet, who continually walks in and out on tiptoe, alternately opens and closes the windows. The Young Man wants to know how to keep memory alive, for otherwise, he says, "It is very difficult to live." And the Old Man tells him, "For that reason one must fly from one thing to another until one loses himself." The Stenographer appears again and tells the Young Man that since her love for him is not returned, she would like to leave the house. When he assures her she may go, she becomes offended and pretends he wants to throw her out. Since there are no letters to write, however, she walks off. The Old Man suspects she is a dangerous woman. But he too leaves when a Friend enters and breezily taking a cocktail, flops on the sofa to boast of his amorous conquests. The Friend tries to humor the Young Man by threatening to drive him into the street, grappling with him, and mocking his obsession. He drinks incessantly, repeats the fact that he never has time for anything, and impatiently watches the clock. The Old Man re-enters angrily, saying, "I shall forget my hat"—translating past into future action, as he had suggested before one must do. When questioned by the Friend, he explains disdainfully, "That is, I have forgotten my hat." When the sound of a thunderstorm approaches, the three hide behind a screen.

A little Boy enters, dressed in white, a candle in one hand and a wounded Cat held by the paw in the other. In the dim light, Cat and Boy speak to each other in delicate verses. Both are awaiting death, which they have pathetically imagined as a carnivorous lizard. When the Cat moves to the door, a hand reaches out from the darkness and takes the animal away. The little Boy chants, "He is sunk./ A hand has taken him;/ It must be the hand of God." The same hand reaches out to take the child.

**137**

The three return from behind the screen, fanning themselves. The Valet enters to report the death of a neighbor's child and the stoning of a cat in the garden. The Young Man speaks of his attempt to conquer obstacles, material things, and to search for the ideal without causing others pain. The Friend scoffs at him for not taking advantage of the moment to gratify his senses, at which the Old Man vehemently interposes. The Friend scoffs at him too, saying an old man cannot understand these things. The Old Man justifies himself: "I have struggled all my life to light a lamp in the darkest places. And when people have tried to twist the neck of the dove, I have caught their hands and helped the dove fly away." To which the Friend adds cynically, "And naturally, the hunter starved to death," and the Young Man comments, "Hunger be blessed."

A Second Friend enters, wearing a suit "of exaggerated cut" with huge blue buttons, his vest and tie made of lace. (The author suggests a very young actor or a girl for this role.) In his delicate child's imagination, the Second Friend strives continually to resurrect the lost happiness of childhood. Except for this, life has no meaning for him. The Old Man thinks him completely mad, and the First Friend contemptuously summarizes it all as "the fear of death." After the others have gone, and after the Stenographer has been told that there is still no work for her, the Young Man is left alone with the Second Friend, who is singing in his sleep:

> *Yo vuelvo por mis alas*
> *dejadme tornar.*
> *Quiero morirme siendo*
> *manantial.*

*Quiero morirme fuera
del mar.*

(I return for my wings,
let me go back.
I want to die being
a spring,
I want to die out of
the sea.)

And so at the end of the act, when the Young Man is told that it is six o'clock "exactly" (the same time as at the beginning of the act), we feel he has surrendered not to the present of living memory, whose illusions he hopes to sustain forever, but rather to his Second Friend's past suicidally cut off from the present by dead memory. He has discarded all his advisers, all his other alter-egos: the Old Man who would "remember toward tomorrow"; the First Friend, who in his avidity to seize the present would "eat the fruit green" and cut the budding flower "to put in my lapel"; and the Stenographer, whom he does not need, his living reminder of the present which is forever ready to succumb to him.

In the second act, the five years of waiting have elapsed. Dressed in a beautiful robe of laces and enormous red bows, the Betrothed has just jumped out of bed at the sound of an automobile horn outside. Opening her balcony window, she invites the Rugby Football Player to climb in. He wears knee-pads and a helmet, and his pockets are stuffed with Havana cigars, which he is constantly lighting and extinguishing. Not saying a word, he casually receives the impetuous girl in his arms. She runs her hands

**139**

over his strong virile body, and compares him with her fiancé, "the old man, the lyric one," marvelling that the Football Player kisses her differently each day. She hugs him and calls him "my dragon," at which he blows smoke in her face. When her fiancé is announced by the Maid, she tells the Football Player to await her outside so that they may elope later in his automobile. Putting on her plainest dress, she meets the Young Man negligently, remarking to her Maid that his cold hand is "waxen and amputated," and that his glance comes apart "like the wing of a dried-up butterfly." He notices the change in her when she asks him if he can play Rugby, or whether he can kill three thousand pheasants in a day. But he embraces her blindly as the fulfillment of his dream. Irked by his "lyricism," she disengages herself saying, "You might have said all that except for the word *dream*. Nobody dreams here." She finally shocks him by remarking that another man has entered her room, and that "a mirror, a table, would be closer to you than I." But what affects him is not her deceit so much as losing the object of his love. "You yourself are not important to me. It's my lost treasure: my love without an object." The stage lights dimmed, he is left alone in the room when the Manikin, dressed in his Betrothed's wedding gown, enters and begins weepingly to sing:

> Yo canto
> muerte que no tuve nunca,
> dolor de velo sin uso,
> un llanto de seda y pluma.
> Ropa interior que se queda
> helada de nieve oscura,
> sin que los encajes puedan

*competir con las espumas.*
*Telas que cubren la carne*
*serán para el agua turbia.*
*Y en vez de rumor caliente,*
*quebrado torso de lluvia.*
*¿Quién usará la ropa buena*
*de la novia chiquita y morena?*

(I sing
the death I never had,
sorrow of the veil unused,
lament of silk and plumes.
Underclothes that remain
frozen with dark snow,
so that the laces can never
play rival to the foam.
Fabrics to cover the body
will be left for muddy water.
Instead of warm murmuring,
a torso broken by rain.
Who will wear the fine dress
of the bride so dark and small?)

The Manikin finds the Young Man at fault, and ascribes his broken engagement to his being "a sleepy lagoon." She urges him on with the warm dream of his beloved's body. But he shouts at her to be silent, since everything has been drowned "in the sands of the mirror." But suddenly she shows him what must be love's consequence, what has escaped his cold memory. It is symbolized by a child's pink little dress which, she says, "I stole from the sewing room."

*Las fuentes de leche blanca*
*mojan mis sedas de angustia*
*y un dolor blanco de abeja*
*cubre de rayos mi nuca.*

**141**

> *Mi hijo. Quiero a mi hijo.*
> *Por mi falda lo dibujan*
> *estas cintas que me estallan*
> *de alegría en la cintura.*
> *Y es tu hijo.*

> (The fountains of warm milk
> moisten my silks with anguish
> and the white sorrow of a bee
> covers my neck with lightning.
> My son. I want my son.
> These bands which mark him
> through my skirt are bursting
> with joy at the waist.
> And he is your son.)

She persuades him to return to the present, which will
rouse at his touch, and to the woman yearning for him in
his house—the Stenographer. With new fervor, he promises the Manikin:

> *Antes que la roja luna*
> *limpie con sangre de eclipse*
> *la perfección de su curva,*
> *traeré temblando de amor*
> *mi propia mujer desnuda.*

> (Before the red moon
> wipes the perfection of its curve clean
> with the blood of eclipse,
> I'll bring my own woman naked
> and trembling with love.)

When the Maid enters the room, the Manikin turns rigid.
Too late, the Old Man comes to warn him, begging him to

begin waiting again. But the Young Man, awakened to the present, disappears in search of the Stenographer.

In the first scene of the third act, a small theatre is inset on the stage, surrounded by a forest. A set of stairs leads up to the inner stage. When the main curtain opens, two black figures, hands and faces painted in plaster of Paris, cross among the treetrunks in the background. A Harlequin, in black and green, carries two masks, alternately putting on one and then the other, always hiding the unused one behind his back. Gesturing in the manner of a ballet performer, he intones the verses appropriate now to the mask "with a very gay expression," now to the one "with a slumbering expression." He sings of time and dream passing, "yesterday and tomorrow eat/ dark flowers of despair," a commentary on the problem of the preceding acts. "Hunting horns" are heard offstage at intervals from this point to the end of the act. A Girl, dressed in a Greek tunic, enters carrying a garland and leaping in the air. She is searching for the lover who waits for her "at the bottom of the sea." The Harlequin tells her "charmingly" that it is a lie. In their poetic colloquy, the Harlequin tries to confuse her, playing on the words "lie" and "truth." This section becomes a variation on the motif of the previous section in which the Manikin's dress would be worn "when the stream marries the sea," and the end of the first act where the Second Friend, mortally afraid of the present, sang, "I want to die being/ a spring,/ I want to die out of/ the sea."

A Clown enters, laughing loudly, his great powdered head shaking like a skull. The Harlequin plays a white violin with golden strings. Both are jesting in the roles they are supposed to play in the circus. When they offer to show the Girl the "fresh algae," "the huge snails," and the "lilies of salt" at the bottom of the sea where her lover is waiting, she becomes "frightened by reality" and leaves weeping. Trumpets are sounded as the Stenographer enters in tennis clothes, accompanied by the First Mask, dressed "in the style of 1900," "poisonous yellow hair falling behind her like a shawl," and wearing a white plaster of Paris mask. The First Mask speaks with "a slight Italian accent." Together they gossip about pretended love affairs, and the Stenographer dreams of her real-life situation reversed: her delighted jilting of the Young Man. She is continually echoing, half ridiculously, half pathetically, earlier speeches made by the Young Man. When the Young Man himself appears, the Harlequin and the Clown intentionally confuse him, and tell him there is no need for further search since the streets are blocked off by the circus in town. When he does finally meet the Stenographer, he sings his newly awakened love for her. Enchanted, she believes it only as a dream.

> *Sí; que el sol es un milano.*
> *Mejor: un halcón de vidrio.*
> *No: que el sol es un gran tronco,*
> *y tú la sombra de un río.*
> *¿Cómo, si me abrazas, dí,*
> *no nacen juncos y lirios?*
> *y no destiñen tus brazos*
> *el color de mi vestido?*
> *Amor, déjame en el monte*
>   *de nube y rocío,*
> *para verte grande y triste,*
>   *un cielo dormido.*

( Yes; for the sun is a bird of prey.
Better: a falcon made of glass.
No: for the sun is a large tree-trunk,
and you, the shadow of a river.
How, if you embrace me,
will not weeds and lilies grow?
and so won't your arms now
fade the color of my dress?
Let me stay on the mountain, love,
    with clouds and dew,
so that I may see you large and sad,
    a sky fallen asleep.)

She pretends to be acting in a play, and insists on mounting the inner stage, its curtain drawn on a reduced version of the Library in the first act. The Young Man wearily follows her. Here she explains that she *has* loved him and *will* love him. The dead little Boy of the first act passes across the stage, and the Young Man thinks of his unborn son. He embraces the Stenographer, who, becoming completely his own echo, tells him, "I will go with you when five years pass." Now his new-found reality has become an inverted dream; he goes off seeking his house, directed by the Old Man, who has suddenly appeared and is obviously pleased by the outcome.

In the second scene of the final act, the Young Man is at home in his library. The Manikin, now without head or hands, is still wearing the forgotten wedding gown. Several suitcases are strewn across the floor. Everything familiar to him has grown quite small: "My house had an enormous patio where I played with my hobby horses. When I was twenty and saw it again, it was so small it seemed to me incredible that I should have been able to fly about in

**145**

it so much." The Young Man orders his Valet to prepare his evening suit and patent leather shoes. After he leaves, "almost like a shadow," to go upstairs to change, three Gamblers enter the house, wearing formal clothes and "long capes of white satin which reach down to their feet." In conspiratorial voices they discuss the pathetic cases of several of their recent "victims" in other countries. When the Young Man reappears in a frock coat, they greet him with sly remarks about his clothes being so elegant he "should not need to disrobe again." They all join in a game of cards, and at the very first deal, when all cards are turned out, the Young Man nervously tries to hold his own back. He seems not to hear their insistent and horrible request that he yield. He tries to forestall them with offers of various liquors. When they tell him, "One must win or lose; come, your card," he sorrowfully throws down the ace of hearts. At the same moment, the ace of hearts "appears, illuminated on the library shelves." One of the Gamblers whips out a pistol and shoots an "arrow" at it. The card disappears and the Young Man puts his hand over his heart. The Gamblers leave hastily. Dying, the Young Man calls to his servant, admitting that everything is now lost. Only two Echoes answer him when he closes his eyes on the sofa. His Valet appears with a lighted candelabrum, and the clock strikes twelve.

Except for the lyric interludes of the Cat and Boy in the first act, of the Manikin and Young Man in the second, and of the Harlequin and Girl in the third, *Así Que Pasen Cinco Años* is almost entirely removed from Lorca's popular dramatic style. The slight narrative seems to groan under the burden of elaborate stage devices. The logical

**146**

dramatic structure begins to disintegrate as the play runs irresolutely, now in the distorted atmosphere of the puppet show, now in the luminous movements of the ballet. The first and second acts, while they are consistent in their use of poetic symbols, are stationary and obscure in their dramatic progression. But the third act is unhinged from the rest in that certain symbolic characters owe their existence on the stage to something outside the immediate argument of the play. Yet there is a striking relevance created in a dimension beyond the poetic, the dramatic, and the pictorial, which is worth examining. It is the relevance of the musical conception. And by "musical conception" is not meant the mere musical supplement to the dramatic involvement, but a subtle thematic organization which seems based on a musical rather than on a dramatic pattern.

In the first act, the Stenographer appears on the stage three times: once when she passes silently by the Young Man and the Old Man; again when she desperately asks to leave the house because the Young Man has refused her love; and again toward the end of the act when she suddenly appears, bag in hand, irrelevantly asking, "Did you call?" This statement and repetition of theme is lost until the end of the second act when, urged on by the Manikin, the Young Man remembers the Stenographer and leaves in search of her. She is introduced again in the third act; gossiping with the First Mask, she adopts many of the Young Man's speeches of the first act; and in conversation now, she reverses the situation of their actual relationship by stating that it is *she* who has jilted *him*. When he finally appears, she insists on enacting their talk on a stage within

147

the main stage, a reduced set of the Young Man's library in the first act. Now it is he who comes to know her yearning for love, and she, symbol of his new-found reality, becomes his old frustrated dream. Their positions are reversed, and using his own words she can now refuse him until "five years pass." Thus too, the Manikin is an alterego of the Stenographer, urging the Young Man to pursue the living present. And likewise, in the third act, the Girl seeking her lover at "the bottom of the sea," who is confused and frightened off by the Harlequin, is another version of the Stenographer-Manikin motif representing the present.

There are also the minor themes of the Second Friend and the Dead Child. For, as was remarked earlier, at the end of the first act, when the Young Man is left pondering his illusion, the only adviser who remains by him is this Second Friend whose life is the past and whose death is the present. This is precisely the broken condition of the Young Man himself in the second scene of the third act, when the only things he can remember with happiness while he awaits the summons of death from the Gamblers are the dusty objects of childhood. The connection between the Young Man and the dead little Boy is perhaps more devious. During the first act, the Boy and Cat interlude is a theme which seems to have no immediate relation to the action. In the first scene of the third act, however, it is suddenly revived when the dead little Boy walks silently across the stage to the sound of an offstage voice crying, "My child!" To this, and as if in echo, the Young Man replies, "Yes, my son," thinking of his unborn child which the Manikin promised him should he succeed in getting a bride.

For the purpose of this play, then, a repetition and enlargement of theme is used, as in a musical composition, for the interweaving of idea, character and movement. By this device, the otherwise static and disparate dramatic form is quickened. The major (Stenographer-Manikin) and minor (Cat-Boy and Second Friend) motifs are logically coherent, and in several places seem even to resolve themselves into counterpoint and fugue. The significant thing to notice is not that the musical conception succeeds where the dramatic would or could not, but that an esthetic relationship has been established between two media which has rarely appeared in the modern theatre. Though there is an important philosophic idea in *Así Que Pasen Cinco Años*, the handling is so delicate as to suggest more a lyric poem than a play. By his prodigious juggler's imagination, Lorca has transformed three fishes into three million fishes to feed a starving multitude. By a minor miracle, he succeeds in duping the most naive as well as the most sophisticated observer; and while this power is with the artist, no audience, though it grumble, can come away from the spectacle hungry.

Concerning Lorca's other "surrealist" play, the unfinished *El Público (The Audience)*, there are many contradictory claims. Some friends of the poet have said that Lorca completed the play's five scenes before his death and that some nameless person now owns the finished manuscript. Others say that having completed only part of it, he permitted two scenes to be published, and left notes for the

149

unfinished portion. At present, however, the evidence is that two fragments did appear: one entitled "Reina Romana" ("The Roman Queen"), the other, "Quinta Escena" ("Fifth Scene"). What these fragments reveal is mainly a prodigious effort to write a play in which the audience itself appears as chief protagonist. There is further proof that it was intended as a violent blast against the commercialized theatre, which Lorca was always combatting. There are glimpses of a merciless, bizarre audience which, piqued at having its wooden conceptions of life broken by the dramatic imagination, would kill the actors and the stage director, while the crucified poet lies dying below. Alfredo de la Guardia quotes Lorca himself as saying of *El Público*, "I don't think there's a company whose enthusiasm could bring it to the stage for an audience to tolerate it without a feeling of outrage." Until the appearance of more conclusive evidence, it is perhaps sufficient to say what the facts themselves imply: of the two worlds of dramatic possibility which Lorca was exploring at this time— the folk and the surrealist—it was fortunate that after learning the limitations implicit in the second, he decided to occupy himself exclusively with the first.

# 6. WOMAN ON THE STAGE—FOLK TRAGEDIES

THE FEW YEARS IMMEDIATELY FOLLOWING THESE EXPERI-
mental works offer the first signs of Lorca's maturity as a
dramatist. The folk tragedies, his best achievement, are the
work of a poet become director-playwright who used
his familiarity with folklore and music to elaborate the
drama's structural design. This multiform talent was the
stuff out of which a reawakened dramatic art emerged.
For his single theme, Lorca went to the folk; and for his
protagonist, he went to woman.

The strength of Lorca's folk drama lies precisely in his
use of woman as bearer of all passion and earthly reality:
the wild superb nature of which Synge had spoken. With
Lorca it is not simply an accidental choice. The Spain
which let its blood for Christ secretly admired the Virgin
more. The Virgin prevailing over all early Spanish church
art was the symbol of earthly fecundity as well as the
mother of divine mercy. The Spaniard often seems to mis-

trust his male saints for not suffering enough or convincingly. Spanish women saints, however, were always known to suffer magnificent and terrible martyrdom. The character of the *dueña,* the woman chaperon, very early became a convention in the Spanish theatre. And she, as the repository of good earthy frankness, knew the world's tricks and provided the audience with the protective motherly domination which it sought in woman. The Don Juan legend has been a popular and recurrent theme in Spanish literature because it re-affirms the generously fertile nature of woman as distinct from the abstract and essentially barren male lover who finds no permanence except in the arms of death. The Spaniard has been somewhat contemptuous of his philandering Don Juan, who instead of conquering women should have been conquering the New World, or even his own small plot of ground.

Lorca's heroines are modern versions of the warm matriarchal type found in all Spanish literature. They are magnetic fields inevitably drawing tragedy to themselves from a too ardent faith in the right of their natural instincts. Again, they are islands which the world cannot touch with its soiled and makeshift logic. Because their humanity is such an extremely procreative answer to life, they threaten to disrupt the mere man-made machinery of social law, which is, finally, a substitution for life. They are the affirmation to the question of the ultimate which man, with the beam of social exigency in his eye, is always begging. When they lose the sense of integration in life which is necessary to them, the world trembles and comes apart. Thus it is as martyrs of frustrated love, from the heroine of *Mariana Pineda,* who dies on the gallows, to the suicide of the youngest daughter in *La Casa de Bernarda Alba,* that Lorca's women uphold the insistent theme of his tragedies.

With increasing subtlety, the musical conception is woven into the dramatic. If *Mariana Pineda* can be compared to a sonata, then *Bodas de Sangre, Yerma,* and *Doña Rosita la Soltera,* constructed with infinitely more complicated motifs, must be compared to concertos. The supplementary use of a musical pattern introduced with *Mariana Pineda* becomes a function integrated in the dramatic form of the latter three. The scene is more variegated, spectacular; the characters multiply, while the principals are more definitely individualized. Only the simplicity of plot with its relentless argument remains the same.

*Bodas de Sangre (Blood Wedding)* was written and produced in Madrid during 1933. Within a few years, it traveled to Latin America, reaching Argentina and Mexico; it was translated into French, English and Russian, and produced in Paris, New York and Moscow. In the original, or where the barriers of translation did not hinder it, its appeal lay in the strong characterization of the peasant struggling with the immutable laws of nature. It tells the story of an unconsummated marriage among the hill folk of Castile. The atmosphere of imagery and speech is transformed with the dry landscape into the repressed emotion of violence which fills the play. A Mother's only remaining son is planning to marry a girl living beyond the hills with her father. Following the recent feud murder of her husband and several sons, the Mother is obsessed with knives and death. The prospective bride, a strong, silent girl "accustomed to solitude," was previously engaged to Leonardo,[1] who is now married to her cousin. But the members of Leonardo's family were guilty of the feud murder. The Mother suspects her son's Betrothed because of the latter's past relationship with Leonardo. And Leonardo, a wild, maladjusted creature, still secretly yearns for the girl he did not marry. The first scene announces the Mother's obsession and the involvement of persons sharing a common destiny.

The second scene is practically a lyrical interlude. It takes place in Leonardo's house where his Mother-in-Law and Wife are putting the children to sleep with a lullaby:

> *Duérmete, rosal,*
> *que el caballo se pone a llorar.*
> *Las patas heridas,*
> *las crines heladas,*
> *dentro de los ojos*
> *un puñal de plata.*
> *Bajaban al río.*
> *¡Ay, cómo bajaban!*
> *La sangre corría*
> *más fuerte que el agua.*

> (Go to sleep, my rosebay,
> for the horse has begun to cry.
> His hoofs wounded,
> his mane frozen,
> a silver dagger
> between his eyes.
> They took him to the river.
> Ay, how they went down!

[1] The only character in the play with a proper name is thus identified with the strength and rapacity of a *lion*.

His blood was flowing
more swiftly than water.)

Leonardo comes in from the fields, irritated by the news of his Wife's cousin's approaching marriage. In his coarse black mood, he leaves his Wife weeping. She spreads her anxiety, enacting it within the verses of the lullaby.

In the third scene, the prospective Groom and his Mother visit the wasteland home of the Betrothed and her father. In conversation, their language becomes clipped like the sandy landscape. When the financial details are discussed and the marriage date is set, they leave. The Betrothed, silent and dutiful till now, suddenly shows her bitterness by biting her own hand. She is physically as strong as a man. Her Maid tells her of the rider who came the night before. The Betrothed is frightened and incredulous. But at that moment, there is the sound of a horse at the window. She looks out. It is Leonardo.

Thus the first act shifts within a dark and light motif: hard imagistic language, natural and colloquial, when people converse together; and symbolic, aerated language when feeling passes into the anonymity of the scene and is translated into poetry. But throughout, the atmosphere is stark, devoid of desire, and the human will is left out. This is the proper emotional setting to a play which turns more and more on a passionate release of the instincts.

The first scene of the second act is in the house of the Betrothed, the morning of her wedding day. She is trying hard to contain herself when, alone and before the other guests, Leonardo enters—a tight root of bitterness. She bids him leave, while the others come singing wedding

songs. When the Groom arrives, she asks him to rush her
off to church, for she is impatient with the pre-nuptial
ceremony while the thought of Leonardo still roams in
her mind:

I want to be your wife, to be with you alone, and not to hear any
voice but yours. And to see none but your eyes. To have you embrace me so tightly that even if my mother, who is dead, should
call me, I could not be separated from you.

This, however, is not said with a lover's passion, but with
the desperation of one who is almost equal to committing
a crime.

The second scene sharpens the conflict between the
social fact of the marriage and the impending irruption
of anarchic instinct. The wedding not yet consummated,
the Groom's Mother joins the talk of the neighbors and
begins to accentuate her characteristic obsession. She
speaks of Leonardo's family as those "handlers of knives
and people of the false smile." Her heightened eloquence
enlarges the images of blood and murder: how she found
one of her sons dead in the square, and how, after touch-
ing the body, "I moistened my hands in his blood and
licked them with my tongue. Because it was my blood."
The Betrothed appears downcast, while Leonardo passes
back and forth across the scene. At the same time that
the main action approaches a climax, the song and talk
of the people grow animated and more naturally lusty
than ever. The Betrothed, who has become increasingly
recalcitrant with her Groom, finally leaves, complaining
of dizziness. Leonardo's Wife, who has the strongest instinct in the matter, finds her husband gone and agonizedly

blurts out her suspicion that the two have run off together. The Groom's Mother violently spurs her son on in pursuit and urges everyone to follow him. There is the smell of blood in the air. She says, "The hour of blood has arrived again. Two camps." It is the hour of tragedy which she has been expecting like the thrust of a blade ever since her first foreboding speech.

The third act turns on the symbolism of song and the strategy of the spectacle. The first scene is a dim forest where two violins are heard playing in the background. It is filled with the supernatural air of a Calderón allegory. Three Woodsmen are singing in verse, like an improvised chorus of fates. They argue the efficacy of the lovers' escape: "One should follow his instinct. They have done well to flee," or "One should follow the road of blood," or "But blood which sees the light is drunk by the earth," or "What then? It is better to die with one's blood flowing than to live with it stagnating." Suddenly the Moon itself enters, dressed as a young woodsman, its white face diffusing a blue light, sorrowing, lost, restless, and singing—the very height of Lorquian moons! "The moon leaves a knife/ abandoned in the air . . ./ How I should like to enter some breast/ that I might warm myself there," it moans. It is a moon made by a child's fairy-tale imagination, of white chalk and eggshell. Then an old Beggar Woman appears—the personification of Death. She describes the pursuit into the forest and commands the Moon to aid her: "Light up the vest and open the buttons,/ and then the knife will know its way." The Groom enters, white with destiny, and she agrees to lead him to Leonardo. The Woodsmen pass again, and echo the impending tragedy. For a moment the scene focuses upon the escaped lovers—a scene which Lorca says should be "full of great sensuality." Accepting the inevitability of their situation and the tragedy to follow, they blame not themselves but the blind lusts which the earth has created in them. They go deeper into the wood to hide. But suddenly, there are two loud cries, and the double murder has been accomplished. The Moon advancing from the background stops short; the music of the violins ceases as the Beggar Woman reappears. She opens her cloak in the center of the stage like a bird with huge wings. Then the blue light of the Moon is shut off.

As it concerns the three main actors, the violence of this scene is human. With the others—the Woodsmen, who are the fates, the Moon, who is the messenger of Death, and the Beggar Woman, who is Death itself— the scene rises to the supernatural plane, suggesting the Greek *deus ex machina*. There is also the growing sense of similarity with the Tristan-Isolde legend, and with the mythologies of all nations that ever boasted a folk to conserve them. The communication runs on two levels: the classical artistic convention, and the folk-legend character of violence and tragedy.

The short final scene, much of it in verse, is the summation of the tragic statement slowly become impersonal. It takes place in a bare massive enclosure suggestive of a church. Two seated girls are winding out a red skein, singing:

> *Jazmín de vestido*
> *cristal de papel.*
> *Nacer a las cuatro,*

> *morir a las diez.*
> *Ser hilo de lana,*
> *cadena a tus pies*
> *y nudo que apriete*
> *amargo laurel.*

> ( Jasmin dress,
> crystal paper.
> Born at four o'clock,
> and dead at ten.
> To be the woolen yarn,
> the chain to your feet,
> and the knot that ties
> your bitter laurel wreath. )

Through their song, these girls spread an atmosphere of transparent lyricism. One feels that they uphold the tragedy through the simplicity of understatement in the words. In another way, these verses are a counterpart of the chorus of Woodsmen in the previous scene. Their extreme delicacy echoes the ageless old melody breathed on the wind at the coming of birth and death. Destiny here is woman. There is no male character in the final scene.

The first recognizable player to enter is Leonardo's Mother-in-Law, who has become nameless and somewhat like all relatives who come when death requires their mourning. Her appearance is a prelude to the more important actors: the Beggar Woman, and the Mother and the Betrothed who follow. The Beggar Woman dissolves the personal tragedy in her description of the double murder in the wood:

**159**

*Yo los vi; pronto llegan; dos torrentes*
*quietos al fin entre las piedras grandes,*
*dos hombres en las patas del caballo.*
*Muertos en la hermosura de la noche.*

. . . . . .

*Los dos cayeron, y la novia vuelve*
*teñida en sangre falda y cabellera.*

. . . . .

*Así fué; nada más. Era lo justo.*
*Sobre la flor del oro, sucia arena.*

(I saw them suddenly appear like two torrents
quiet at last among the huge rocks:
two men buried in the horse's hoofs.
Dead in the beautiful calm of night.

. . . . . .

Both fallen, and the betrothed returning,
her skirt and hair stained with blood.

. . . . . .

And so it was; nothing more. It was just.
Over the flower of gold, dirty sand.)

When the Mother hears a neighbor weeping, she is an-
noyed; her own tears are dry. Now all her sons are dead.—

Your tears are only tears of the eyes—nothing more; and mine will
come when I am alone, from the soles of my feet, from my roots,
and will be more fiery than blood.

Out of my dream I shall make a cold dove of ivory, bearing camel-
lias of frost over the cemetery. But no; not "cemetery," not "cemetery": bed of earth, bed which protects them and wafts them to
heaven.

**160**

For her, the death of her last son ends the earth's terrible hunger for blood. The ritual now accomplished, her knowledge can no longer bring her pain. What should she care, therefore, for the protestations of the Betrothed, who comes to her now, wanting to die—to die so that the world may be convinced of her innocence and "honor."

What does your honor mean to me? What does your death mean to me? What does anything matter to me any more? Blessed be the leaves of grain because my sons are beneath them; blessed be the rain because it washes the faces of the dead; God be blessed, who lays us down together to rest.

Death is constantly washing the accumulation of personal grief away from the cloth of life; it cannot bring more tragedy than that. Yet, the acceptance of death on these terms is seen less through Catholic morality than through the knowledge of biological ritual. Lorca wished to take abstract death and the passage to heaven out of thought, and to substitute the knowledge of death in everything directly perceptible on earth. He does not enlarge his symbols of decay. For death, like life itself, is neither foul nor ugly: it is only the withering of strong mountainous things and weak colorful things. Weighing Catholic morality as it is conventionally preached, Lorca finds that it does not safeguard the innocent of spirit. On the contrary. Innocence invites a terrible fate which not even martyrdom can sanctify. In the deed itself, life is minimized, endangered, and finally atrophied. What exists in man and all of nature is that perfection of sensual reality which needs no compensation in an afterlife. Perhaps of death, then, it is only possible to say with the Beggar

161

Woman, "It was just. Over the flower of gold, dirty sand."

For the first time, with *Bodas de Sangre,* one can speak of Lorca as poetic dramatist rather than as dramatic poet. Action is no longer static, nor congealed in the frames of "three prints." To be sure, there are evidences of a lyricism seeking to arrest the action in the lullaby scene of the first act; later in the forest scene with the Woodsmen, Moon and Beggar Woman; and finally in the first part of the last scene where the seated girls sing to their weaving. But these are not interludes which have been created as ends in themselves; rather, they operate as a respectable dramatic device: as projectors of the action on an inner screen, catching all the emotion previously rehearsed by the actors. Moreover, the central motifs are emphasized by economy of symbols and imagery in these scenes: the horse, the knife, the stream, the flow of blood. Likewise, spectacular and supernatural effects like the personification of Moon, Death, and Fates, add to the conciseness of dramatic statement. From the standpoint of the play's imaginative development, they are not artifices by which extra-human forces intrude into the dramatic situation, as in the old Greek tragedy. Rather, they serve to indicate most powerfully the fate which the human actors have been nursing in themselves from the very beginning. Death is the personal creation of each character and not a masked figure in sanctified descent from a hidden scaffold above.

Those who criticized *Bodas de Sangre* as typical of the lyric poet's deviations on the stage, were actually blind to the significance of the dramatist's intention. Far from being an amateur playwright, Lorca was exploring the primitive dramatic structure, the Catholic mass, the tribal ritual, and attempting thereby to create a tragic form which might fit the modern condition without relinquishing the spontaneity of the ancient. No mere poetic trickster would prescribe such an arduous discipline for himself in the theatre; nor could any poet simulate it who was not aware of some impelling drive to universalize his art. Though touched by every man, tragedy can be re-created only by those whose imagination, born of a sense of mass and weight in human suffering, is continually being purified in the struggle against it.

Written and produced in 1934, the year following *Bodas de Sangre*, *Yerma* [1] is Lorca's first tragedy constructed on a broad base of dramatic realism. Whereas the characters of *Bodas de Sangre* are dominated by a common sense of sharing a tragic fate (where the blind action of lust which results in tragedy arises from the earth, involving everyone in its consequences), the whole tragic burden in *Yerma* is borne by a single woman, and is measured by the deepening of her struggle with the problem of frustrated motherhood. While *Bodas de Sangre* follows in the tradition of Lope de Vega, who insisted on the spectacular and collective conception of tragic action, *Yerma* follows in the tradition of Calderón de la Barca, who insisted on the individual conception of tragedy, formulated by a religious code setting certain moral bounds to action. This makes not only for a natural difference in dramatic construction, but for the resolution of tragedy on a higher spiritual plane in *Yerma* than in *Bodas de Sangre*.

[1] Literally translated, *yerma* is *desert, sterility*.

**163**

Although there is less verse in *Yerma* than in any other
Lorca play,[1] the author still insists, in his subtitle, on its
essential poetic character: "A Tragic Poem in Three Acts
and Six Scenes." When the curtain rises on the first scene,
Yerma is found asleep with her needlework at her feet.
Bathed in a strange white light, the scene portrays the
last moment of her dream: a shepherd crosses on tiptoe,
leading a child by the hand. The two regard the sleeping
figure for a moment till a clock strikes. When they leave,
the light changes "into the happy light of a spring morning." Whereupon Yerma wakes. This bit of stage décor
effectively introduces the character of Yerma and the
whole motif of the tragedy. With the first few speeches
in the home of Juan and Yerma, the source of tragedy is
opened wide. The theme of fecundity and death, love and
marriage, as symbolized in Yerma and Juan, is vividly
announced. Yerma is a malleable, richly poetic girl, but
frank and definite in her need. She opposes the earth
which Juan is working as an energetic farmer. She is herself the earth. Juan does not like to be reminded of her
desire for a child. Because he is impotent, he cannot actually "see" her. She, on the other hand, sees everything.
And this is the tragedy of her life: that what she sees,
though simple, is unmitigated; and that her need for a
child, though natural, is unsatisfied and begins to obsess
her like a disease. Further, Yerma's friend María, a simple
peasant girl, is introduced. She is going to have a child
and Yerma is delighted and more excited than María herself. There is a lovely pathos in the advice she gives María:
"Don't walk about too much and when you breathe
breathe as softly as if you had a rose between your teeth."

[1] This was written before *Bernarda Alba* was published.

Towards the end of the scene, Victor appears. He is a shepherd, robust, physically attractive. (And Victor's appearance seems like a re-entrance, for he suddenly becomes identified with the dream-shepherd of the beginning.) He hints at her preoccupation: her desire for a child and her fear of Juan's frigidity. Already we come to see Juan as the symbol of the materialist, the blind provider. There is some sense too that Yerma is drawn to Victor in a way she cannot account for. Her eyes linger over the spot where he has been standing. And while spinning alone, she sings to the child of her imagination:

> ¿De dónde vienes, amor, mi niño?
> "De la cresta del duro frío."
> ¿Qué necesitas, amor, mi niño?
> "La tibia tela de tu vestido."
> ¡Que se agiten las ramas al sol
> y salten las fuentes alrededor!
>
> * * *
>
> ¿Qué pides, niño, desde tan lejos?
> "Los blancos montes que hay en tu pecho."
>
> * * *
>
> ¿Cuándo, mi niño, vas a venir?
> "Cuando tu carne huela a jazmín."
> ¡Que se agiten las ramas al sol
> y salten las fuentes alrededor!
>
>
> (Where do you come from, love, my child?
> "From the heights of bitter cold."
> What do you need, love, my child?
> "The warm cloth of your dress' folds."
> Let the branches shake in the sun
> and the fountains leap about us!
>
> * * *

What do you ask for, my child, so far?
"The white mountains of your breasts."

.    .    .    .    .    .

When are you coming, my child?
"When your flesh smells of jasmin."
Let the branches shake in the sun
and the fountains leap about us!

In the second scene the dramatic complications are well under way. Yerma has a long passionate talk with an old peasant woman—Lorca's name for her is simply the old Pagan Woman—twice married and bearer of fourteen sons. A powerful creature, her nature is full of deep earth roots. Yerma has been married three years now and is still childless. The Pagan Woman, who senses the tragedy, is silent. Yerma keeps questioning her, however, and is answered cautiously, in hints. The Pagan Woman asks whether Yerma loves her husband. Yerma does not know, but exclaims, "God will aid me." At this, the old woman turns on her abruptly:

When are you going to realize that he does not exist? Only man can help you. But there should be a God, even a very tiny one, to send lightning down on those men whose seed is rotten and who puddle up the happiness of the fields.

It is a strong denunciation of Juan, and the Pagan Woman leaves on this. But Yerma understands that there is no solution for her in the experience of others.

Then two young women enter. Like Yerma, they have come to carry food to their husbands working in the fields. The First Woman has left her child asleep at home. Immediately Yerma's anxiety is aroused. "Children must not

**166**

be left alone. Are there pigs about your house?" And the surprised mother rushes off at Yerma's alarming suggestion. The Second Woman, who is recently married and without children, pokes fun at her. She admits no interest whatever in having children. Yerma tells her she is only a frilly little girl. Frilly, yes, the Woman answers; but she didn't want to marry in the first place; she was forced into it. Marriage is an imposition of the old upon the young. She would much rather play in clear streams, ring bells, and occasionally take a drink of anisette. She rushes off laughing when Victor enters, singing a shepherd's song:

> *¿Por qué duermes solo, pastor?*
> *¿Por qué duermes solo, pastor?*
> *En mi colcha de lana*
> *dormirás mejor.*

> (Why, shepherd, do you sleep alone?
> Why, shepherd, do you sleep alone?
> You'd sleep much better
> in my warm wool cover.)

And Yerma picks up the refrain directly:

> *Los robles ponen agujas, pastor,*
> *debajo de tu almohada, pastor,*
> *y si oyes voz de mujer*
> *es la rota voz del agua, pastor, pastor.*

> (Beneath your pillow, shepherd,
> the oaks stick needles, shepherd;
> if you hear a woman's voice there,
> it's the broken call of waters, shepherd.)

The intimate short dialogue which follows discloses an inner struggle to contain their deepest feelings for each other. Victor, it is clear, is Yerma's natural mate. They speak to each other like children: lightly, hearts in their mouths. Each senses in the other what cannot be expressed. Yerma is certain, unafraid, looking deeply into him, when Juan approaches. Juan suspects immediately, harshly upbraids Yerma, and sends her home.

The poles have been established in the first act. Yerma already realizes the tragedy of frustration in her relations with Juan. She seeks desperately to find meaning and efficacy, because she cannot easily yield to despair. Yet she must run the narrow circle about her again and again until, exhausted, she returns in the end to herself to find that her only knowledge is in the deed.

The first scene of the second act develops the implications of the preceding action. A group of peasant women washing by a stream discuss Yerma's plight and state a new development: Juan has brought his two old-maid sisters to his house to watch over Yerma. The Washerwomen, who provide the only immediate social setting to a play turning more and more about an individual, are divided in their opinions. They all see the tragedy; some blame Juan and others, Yerma. The Sisters-in-Law themselves come in and wash silently. Then there is a deep sensual singing:

> Por el monte ya llega
> mi marido a comer.
> Él me trae una rosa
> y yo le doy tres.

*Por el llano ya vino*
*mi marido a cenar.*
*Las brasas que me entrega*
*cubro con arrayán.*

*Por el aire ya viene*
*mi marido a dormir.*
*Yo alhelíes rojos*
*y él rojo alhelí.*

*Hay que juntar flor con flor*
*cuando el verano seca la sangre del segador.*

(Down the mountain my husband
is coming to eat.
He brings me a rose
and I bring him three.

Through the fields
my husband came in to dine.
The hot coals he brings me
I cover with myrtle.

Through the night air my husband
is coming to sleep.
He like a gillyflower red
and I like red gillyflowers.

When summer saps the blood of the sower,
then let us join our flowers together. )

The women continue their songs in the rhythm of fertility, accentuating Yerma's isolation. They can hardly imagine a barren woman.

In the second scene it is twilight in Yerma's house. Juan

is seated, attended by his two sisters. Here the emotional restraint contrasts sharply with the songs of the Washerwomen in the previous scene. Juan is seen more clearly, in a light becoming hard and austere. The Sisters-in-Law begin to move about in the background like ghosts. When Yerma comes in the conversation between her and Juan is clipped and full of violent repressed feeling. Estrangement has opened like a chasm between them. Yerma cannot live in stoical forbearance, which she regards as deathly. Still, the word from everybody is "humility," "acceptance"—but she cannot accept what is without passion or fruit. This knowledge is a little maddening for her.

> ¡Ay, qué prado de pena!
> ¡Ay, qué puerta cerrada a la hermosura!,
> que pido un hijo que sufrir, y el aire
> me ofrece dalias de dormida luna.
> Estos dos manantiales que yo tengo
> de leche tibia son en la espesura
> de mi carne dos pulsos de caballo
> que hacen latir la rama de mi angustia.
> ¡Ay, pechos ciegos bajo mi vestido!
> ¡Ay, palomas sin ojos ni blancura!
> ¡Ay, qué dolor de sangre prisionera
> me está clavando avispas en la nuca!
> Pero tú has de venir, amor, mi niño,
> porque el agua da sal, la tierra fruta,
> y nuestro vientre guarda tiernos hijos,
> como la nube lleva dulce lluvia.

> (Oh, what a field of pain!
> Oh, what a door shut on loveliness!
> When I ask a child for my suffering, the wind
> gives me dahlias from a sleeping moon.
> These two streams of warm milk

**170**

I possess become in the closeness
of my flesh two quiverings of a horse
which make my branch of anguish beat.
Oh, blind breasts beneath my dress!
Oh, eyeless doves of no whiteness!
Oh, such sorrow of imprisoned blood
sticking wasps to my neck!
But you must come, love, my child,
because water yields salt, and earth fruit,
and our belly holds dear children
as clouds bear sweet rain.)

Later María comes with her child, saying she has been afraid to visit heretofore because of Yerma's envy. Yerma explains that it is not envy but her feeling of poverty. And the fixation of five years is now turning to the conviction that "I shall end by believing that I myself am my own child." She feels humbled by the fertility about her:

Yes, I am offended, offended and forever humbled, seeing how the wheat grows tall, how the fountains never cease flowing and how the sheep give birth to hundreds of lambs, and the dogs, and it seems that the whole field is suddenly standing on its toes to show me its lovely dozing creatures, while I feel two hammer blows here instead of the mouth of my child.

María is a natural woman who grows uneasy listening to Yerma. Victor is a natural man with a fine instinct, but he cannot answer Yerma. She seeks an answer; and Juan knows it, but infers that she wishes to dishonor him morally thereby. He therefore forbids her to leave the house. But at the end of the act, seeking a supernatural source, she goes to the Conjurer.

We see this act clearly in two terms: the Christian sym-

bol of work and order, which is the world of Juan, María
and Victor, and the pagan world of passion, which is disorder—all of nature—and the sensual landscape of Yerma's imagination. She is being forced into a martyred
position which is obnoxious to her. She seeks efficacy
from life, not fermentation or glory, since she cannot con-
ceive that the functions of man are other than the functions of nature. Her obligation is to herself, a conscience
which will not allow her an artificial solution to the problem.

In the third act, Yerma learns from the Conjurer about
women who have borne children with supernatural aid.
She is told of a woman who stood in the river, "with her
shoes and petticoats drenched in blood . . . but her face
shining," and conceived. Yerma's idea of child-bearing is
a mixture of milk and light: a pure form. Her reality is
the whole of inviolable nature existing within her; but
when ghostly frigidity is placed there instead, she would
tear it out rather than have it sit on her heart. Her relation to Juan is that of a mountain of fire to a mountain
of frost. But she has her honor: "I don't love him, I don't
love him, and still he is my only salvation. For honor and
chastity, my only salvation." Dawn comes and Juan enters
with his two sisters. He accuses her of dishonoring him
out of doors. Yerma defends herself simply and unanswer-
ably, as a woman:

Draw close to me and smell my clothing; come, come close! See if
you can find an odor that is not yours, that has not partaken of your
body. Take me nude, stand me in the middle of the street and spit
on me. Do with me what you wish, for I am your wife, but be care-
ful not to insinuate another man's name between my breasts.

# WOMAN ON THE STAGE—FOLK TRAGEDIES

But what bothers Juan is that "the people will begin to talk" about her wanderings. And when he asks what she is looking for, she embraces him passionately:

I am looking for you. I am looking for you; I seek you day and night without finding a shade to breathe in. It is your blood and your help I want.

This goes against the grain; he throws her away from him. Now she sees herself, frustrated, really seeking herself. She cries, "Cursed be my father who left me his father's blood of a hundred children. Cursed be my blood which seeks them knocking against the walls." Then her final outburst reveals the crux of the whole play:

It is one thing to want something with the head and another thing is when the body—cursed be the body!—does not answer us. It is all written down somewhere and I am not going to begin fighting the seas with my bare hands. So it is! Let my mouth be struck dumb!

From this point on, one expects only the extremest consequences of frustration—suicide or murder. Yerma commits both.

The last scene is enacted at a mountain shrine where women have come to pray for children. As night falls, Yerma is there watching the celebration of a popular masque. It is played by two women: one disguised as "a robust male," and the other as "a fertile female." Some children who are present immediately recognize the characters as The Devil and His Wife. Singing duets in the rhythm of the popular ballad, the "man" grasps a bull's horn in each hand, and the woman, a collar of bells. Lorca cautions against an exaggerated interpretation of this scene: "These characters should not be made to seem in the least grotesque, but of great beauty, as products of the pure earth." Guitars ring out. There is the smell of a primitive fertility rite, the lost art of peoples which flourished before the spread of tribes into towns—a heavy, steady, fiery music of flesh and earth.

The old Pagan Woman reappears to tell Yerma what she could not before, when Yerma was a young wife. Juan is to blame, she says, and Juan's whole family, for

. . . neither his father, nor his grandfather, nor his great-grand-father behaved like pure-blooded men. For them to have sons, it has been necessary that heaven and earth meet—they were made with spit . . . On the other hand, your family, no! You have brothers and cousins a hundred miles around. See what a curse has been thrown over your loveliness.

The Pagan Woman adds that her son is waiting nearby.

My house needs a woman. Go with him and all three of us shall live together. . . . If you enter my house you will still find the odor of cradles there. The ashes of your quilt will turn to bread and salt for your children. Come. Don't worry about what people will say.

Yerma, however, who knows the responsibility of form, of honor, cannot abide by this. She upbraids the old woman sharply and concludes, "Mine is a sorrow which has already departed from the flesh." Thus her frustration seems to have turned almost into mysticism. She is a woman who has gone the complete round of her being, until she is "inverted." She is ready for anything, yet not in her old way, if she do it now, as she must, but in a way

**174**

that is suddenly revealed to her. The old Pagan leaves in search of some other woman for her son.

When Yerma moves, she discovers that Juan has been spying behind a rock. The ensuing scene is short, with words and images that are sharp direct arrows aimed at the tragic center. There is no pretense between them. Juan comes to give her his grief, to bring her back to his ashen life once and for all: "The moment has finally come to throw off this continual lamentation after obscure things, things outside of life, things empty as air." Outside of life, things of no substance? Yerma replies with anger and amazement. It is her very core he is denying, full of life and substance. Yet, they do not concern him: "What is important to me is what I have in my hands, what I see with my eyes." But this is just what Yerma has been waiting to hear from him. "It's true," she cries, suddenly capturing the significance of the tragedy, "one does not know the truth when it is wrapped up inside, but how huge it is and how it cries when it walks out and raises its arms!" But he is dumb to her catastrophic meaning. "Life is sweeter without children . . . I am happy not having them." What then do you want of me? Yerma asks. You, yourself, he answers. But finally she sees him clearly, and defines his words: "That's it! You want a house, peace, and a wife. But nothing more. Isn't that so?" And Juan agrees. Never has he really been troubled about her desire for a child—his own impotence admitted or not; it has meant nothing to him. Now she is equal to the deed. At last she knows her silence broken, her answer given to her. Juan moves close to kiss her. I am searching for you, he says, echoing her words. No, Yerma replies, you

**175**

search for me only when you are hungry, "when you feel like eating a bird." And knowing now the final betrayal and no answer, she chokes him for his impurity which is worse than the desert he has imposed upon her. She kills him with her own hands, cleanly, with the strength of her passion.

A chorus of women approaches. Yerma, relieved of her burden, says:

I'm going to rest without ever waking anxiously to see whether my blood has announced the coming of new blood. My body barren forever. What would you know? Don't come near me, because I have killed my child. I myself have killed my child!

Having killed him, she has also committed suicide within herself; for according to her self-created code, she is at last certain, now that her husband is dead, never to bear children.

In both the moral and dramatic sense, *Yerma* is the highest achievement of Lorca's theatre. The character of Yerma rises out of the anonymity of a universal problem into real tragic stature. Lorca has departed in this play from the use of merely the elementary fact of historical statement as found in *Mariana Pineda;* he has shown resolution in terms of consistently self-impelled motivation. Thus, *Yerma* is not simply an expanded ballad, but a consciously created drama with a beginning, a middle, and an end. The supernatural has become an organic part of the whole. When he employs chorus and dance here, it is a technique integrated with every movement of the plot, so that even Yerma's final resolution, the murder of Juan, gathers impetus if not immediate inspiration from the dionysiac ritual at the shrine in the last scene. There is no quality of emotional expression in this drama which is false to, and which does not find basis in, the immediate character of the land.

In any other context, the murder would be highly grotesque, if not incomprehensible. If it were not an act of passion, then, or if it were not a compulsion rising from a free identification with the land, the whole meaning of the drama would be lost. But Yerma's character and situation, if they are nothing else, are consistent and meaningful. They create a logic of circumstance which becomes absolute on its own terms. If she could have accepted any other terms, of course, Yerma's violence would not have been inevitable. For she might have become reconciled to her plight by yielding to the standardized stoicism of the society about her. She might even have turned further into the bare emotion of Catholic humility or the conviction of martyrdom, as Mariana Pineda did—except that in her own situation, Yerma could not possibly reap the social recognition which was Mariana's reward. On the other hand, she might have chosen to accept the suggestion of the old Pagan Woman, or even of a more conscious Victor, and having left Juan for another, forsaken the moral conventions of society, as the Betrothed did in *Bodas de Sangre*. Only her unique conception of honor made none of these contingencies possible. She sought out all the forms of efficacy, both natural and supernatural, which her own sense of decency might sanction. But when these did not avail, only her unmet passion remained to dictate the extremity of her action. Her law

**177**

was not the mere self-constituted amorality of the anarchist which concludes that since God does not exist, everything is possible; but the tragic form of truth which is as instinctive and imaginative as a poem's.

In her flight from frustrated struggle, Yerma gains nobility and is raised above vain tears. In being poetic, Yerma's solution is an act of creative liberation and an ultimate criticism of Spanish stoical morality. She proves that stoicism is a philosophy suited to a people or to an individual enslaved, for whom the world has grown too large. Instead of fortifying the soul, stoicism extracts the soul and makes it a dead letter in the name of perverted vanity. For the human being who must find some excuse for breathing in and breathing out, life becomes a biological pulp finally dissolved in the earth. Yerma, for whom the world is rich and intimate, is an island of green in a vast sea of stoicism—an island which we feel the angry sea always takes by storm.

Lorca's last dramatic production, *Doña Rosita la Soltera, o el Lenguaje de las Flores* (*Doña Rosita the Spinster, or the Language of the Flowers*), was staged in December, 1935, in Madrid. Subtitled "A Poem of 1900 Granada, Divided into Various Gardens, with Scenes of Song and Dance," the play is actually created out of the living Granadine circumambience. In this it resembles *Mariana Pineda,* of which it is the more mature and more human counterpart. Again, it is a "period" drama, its three acts covering the years 1890–1910. Of the exquisite *la mode,* the flourish of styles and the decadence of gardens, it presents still another version of frustrated love.

**178**

But now it is the frustration created by society's standardized conception of how the individual reacts in an apparent dilemma, though there is, in fact, no initial sense of dilemma in the individual. The bourgeois setting at the turn of the century frames a heroine, Doña Rosita, who lives within her drawing room and suffers like a wilting flower for twenty years. And yet, though she seldom stirs outside the house and garden, her plight reveals the small perishable fragility which is the romantically frustrated life of a woman in the provinces.

The whole action is confined to a parlor overlooking a botanical hothouse in the home of Doña Rosita's foster parents. The occupants of the house besides Doña Rosita are her Uncle, a preoccupied floriculturist; a Housekeeper with an enduring peasant soul, full of folk aphorisms and a swift boisterous feeling for life; and an Aunt, inheritor of the family tradition, a provincial lady with a slightly nervous, bird-like sense of order and decency. The first act, which is all atmosphere and music, moves with the bold flashes of the Housekeeper's personality. It is she, for instance, who scorns flowers and prefers fruit: "For me, flowers smell like a dead child, or like a nun's business, or like church altars. Like sad things. Where there is an orange or a good quince, you can throw out all the roses in the world." And when the Aunt replies disdainfully, "You only want to eat them!" the Housekeeper answers in the folk idiom:

> *La boca sirve para comer,*
> *las piernas sirven para la danza*
> *y hay una cosa de la mujer . . .*

**179**

(The mouth is used for eating,
the legs are used for dancing,
and there is a woman's certain thing . . .)

—at which point she is, of course, stopped by the Aunt's crossing herself desperately.

The Aunt is instrumental in urging her nephew, Rosita's lover, to leave for Perú and his father's estate, where he is bound to make a fortune. Rosita is a naive and graceful figure, mirroring the charm of a romantically languid Granada. With vague palpitations, she receives the news of her lover's intended departure and his promise to return. Together in the parlor, their faces set "vis-à-vis" as in a delicately enamelled cameo, the music of Czerny in the background, they suggest a sweetly vaporous romance, speaking to each other in verses of fragile "sweet-nothings." When he leaves, and Rosita hears the approach of her Uncle, she dries her tears, and opening a book to a page which he has previously indicated to her, she reads the description of the Mutable Rose:

> *Cuando se abre en la mañana*
> *roja como sangre está;*
> *el rocío no la toca*
> *porque se teme quemar.*
> *Abierta en el mediodía*
> *es dura como el coral,*
> *el sol se asoma a los vidrios*
> *para verla relumbrar.*
> *Cuando en las ramas empiezan*
> *los pájaros a cantar*
> *y se desmaya la tarde*
> *en las violetas del mar,*
> *se pone blanca con blanco*

de una mejilla de sal;
y cuando toca la noche
blando cuerno de metal
y las estrellas avanzan
mientras los aires se van,
en la raya de lo oscuro
se comienza a deshojar.

(In the morning unfolding,
red it is like blood.
Afraid of burning,
dew does not touch it.
At noon, it is wide open
and hard as coral.
Sun peeks through glass
to see it shine.
When birds in the branches
begin to sing,
and afternoon faints
in the violet tints of sea,
it turns white, white
as a cheek of salt;
and when night is struck
by a soft metallic horn,
and stars advance
as breezes go,
on the boundary line of darkness,
its petals begin to fall.)

Throughout the first act, ballads like this one serve as dramatic projectors to such effect that there is no question of sugary sentimentality about the main characters. Other ballads, both choral and in dialogue, celebrate the rivers and gallants of Granada. The supplements of music and dance abate the tension of highly geared feminine emotion and delicately re-echo a bitter-sweet romantic era.

In the second act, fifteen years have passed. The action, now crowded with little things, is kaleidoscopic with people's talk. Beginning on a realistic note, it gyrates in the end to an almost grotesque puppetry. A Professor of Political Economy is found in the drawing room, discussing the questions of the day with Rosita's Uncle. "The century which we have just entered will be a materialist century." There is a cocksureness about the Professor, suggesting a caricature of the early scientific determinist attitude. On the subject of mechanical speed, he says enthusiastically, "My friend, Sr. Longoria of Madrid, has just bought an automobile with which he hurls himself along at the fantastic speed of eighteen miles an hour." When the Uncle questions him about a recent automobile race which had to be suspended because all the drivers were killed before reaching their destination, the Professor answers calmly:

Count Zboronsky, who died in the accident, and Marcel Renault, or Renol, since it is customary and possible to say it both ways, also dead in the accident, are martyrs of science who will be enshrined on the day when the religion of positivism arrives.

The Uncle's views are humbler, though he is burningly proud of his botany. The Professor condescends to admire the flowers, though he boasts the superiority of mechanical things. When the Professor leaves, the Housekeeper hints that he might become Rosita's suitor. There is a grand colloquy between the Aunt and the Housekeeper; the latter, unable to understand Rosita's patience, crackles with typical Andalusian irony: "Sometimes I feel like throwing a shoe at her head . . . Because with so much gazing at the sky, she will get to have the eyes of a cow." She and the Aunt begin to quarrel when each questions the measure of the other's devotion to Rosita. Precipitated suddenly, the dispute forces them both to tears. But the breakdown and quick reconciliation between the two is natural and charmingly realistic, suggesting as it does how such things are apt to occur—all in a few moments.

There is a nervous undercurrent established, however, which prepares for a changed Rosita. The peaceful Uncle himself says philosophically, "A moment comes when persons living together many years make of the most trivial things a pretext for annoyance and disturbance, just to give intensity and anxiety to what is definitely dead." The ugly little streak of boredom has only now begun to invade the house. When Rosita enters, her first thought is to ask for the mail, since she is obviously still awaiting news from her lover. She is going to cut a rose for her saint, and the Uncle remarks it is like cutting one of his fingers. Rosita inquires about the mail carrier again, and irritated by the Housekeeper's lapsing indirectness mutters, "In this house there is a little drop of bitterness toward everything." Then in reply to the Aunt's attempt to console her, she explains:

When I don't see people I am happy, but since I must see them . . . And yet it is only in the street that I notice how time passes and I don't want to lose my illusions.

**183**

Now the Aunt shifts to the Housekeeper's argument and suggests that Rosita forget her cousin and think of a new engagement. But Rosita, still warmed by her illusions, will not hear of it.

Three bizarre Old Maids enter with their Mother, wearing exaggerated hats and huge hanging fans. The Old Maids form a chorus of one attitude: the soft hysteria of frustration. Their Mother talks endlessly and pointlessly, and is continually being distracted by her own words. She has brought Rosita a birthday card which represents "a girl dressed in rose, who is at the same time a barometer." She delights in the invention: "The monk with his cassock is much too common nowadays. In keeping with the humidity, the girl's skirt, which is of the finest paper, opens or closes." At this point, the two frilly daughters of Ayola, a neighboring photographer, enter. The Housekeeper announces them: "Here are their highnesses, the great ladies of Ayola, photographer to His Majesty and gold medal at the Madrid exposition." They are a lively and effective contrast to the three starched Old Maids. Throughout the scene they are on the point of bursting into laughter, and their humor affects even Rosita. They brazenly admit that the only reason they love Rosita is that she has a sweetheart: "Women without sweethearts are undercooked, overcooked and all of them . . . well, not all, but some of them . . . In the end, all of them have hydrophobia!" Then the song, "The Language of the Flowers," is sung by Rosita, the three Old Maids and their Mother, and is danced by the Ayola girls. Its central theme is the same as the song of the Mutable

**184**

Rose previously introduced and now orchestrated with
additional verses about other flowers which the company
interposes. It is a charming garden-piece in Lorca's best
manner, strongly reminiscent of Arabic-Andalusian poetry,
and evocative of the period when maidens used to con-
jure their loves with the obscure symbolism of mementos:

> Madre, llévame a los campos
> con la luz de la mañana
> a ver abrirse las flores
> cuando se mecen las ramas.
> Mil flores dicen mil cosas
> para mil enamoradas,
> y la fuente está contando
> lo que el ruiseñor se calla.
>
> .    .    .    .
>
> Sólo en ti pongo mis ojos
> —el heliotropo expresaba—
> "No te querré mientras vivas,"
> dice la flor de la albahaca.
> "Soy tímida," la violeta.
> "Soy fría," la rosa blanca.
> Dice el jazmín: "seré fiel,"
> y el clavel: "¡apasionada!"
> El jacinto es la amargura;
> el dolor, la pasionaria;
> el jaramago, el desprecio
> y los lirios, la esperanza.
> Dice el nardo: "soy tu amigo,"
> "creo en ti," la pasionaria.
> La madreselva te mece,
> la siempreviva te mata.
> Siempreviva de la muerte,
> flor de las manos cruzadas;

**185**

*¡qué bien estás cuando el aire*
*llora sobre tu guirnalda!*

. . . . .

*Sobre tu largo cabello*
*gimen las flores cortadas.*
*Unas llevan puñalitos,*
*otras fuego y otras agua.*
*Las flores tienen su lengua*
*para las enamoradas.*
*Son celos el carambuco;*
*desdén esquivo la dalia;*
*suspiros de amor el nardo,*
*riso la gala de Francia.*
*Las amarillas son odio;*
*el furor, las encarnadas;*
*las blancas son casamiento*
*y las azules, mortaja.*
*Madre, llévame a los campos*
*con la luz de la mañana*
*a ver abrirse las flores*
*cuando se mecen las ramas.*

(Mother, take me to the meadows
in the early morning light
to see the flowers opening
at the fluttering of the boughs.
A thousand flowers tell a thousand things
to a thousand girls in love,
and the fountain is relating
what the nightingale won't sing.

. . . . .

"My eyes are just for you"
—is what the heliotrope means—
"I'll never love you while you're alive,"
the sweet basil flower cries.

"I'm shy," the violet.
"I'm cold," the white rose.
The jasmin says, "I'll be true,"
and the carnation, "Passionate!"
The hyacinth stands for bitterness,
for sorrow, the passion flower,
hedge mustard for contempt,
and lilies for hopefulness.
The spikenard says, "I'm your friend,"
"I believe in you," the passion flower.
The honeysuckle soothes you,
the everlasting kills you.
Everlasting is for death,
flower of the crossed hands;
how beautiful you are when the wind
goes weeping over your wreath!

. . . .

In your long, long hair
cut flowers are whining.
Some carry little knives,
some fires, others water.
The caraway for jealousy,
for cold disdain, the dahlia,
for sighs of love, the spikenard,
the French wild rose for laughter.
Yellow flowers stand for hate,
carmine ones for rage,
white ones for a marriage
and blue ones for the grave.
Mother, take me to the meadows
in the early morning light
to see the flowers opening
at the fluttering of the boughs. )

**The song concluded, the Mother enthusiastically adds that
her daughters also know "the language of the fan . . . of
the gloves . . . of the stamps . . . of the hours . . ."**

**187**

Now the mail carrier finally arrives with a letter from Rosita's sweetheart. In it, the sweetheart announces his decision to marry her. But since he cannot come immediately, he is suggesting a marriage by proxy. The Housekeeper is puzzled: "Good, but 'by proxy,' what does that mean?" Rosita explains, but the Housekeeper is not satisfied: "And what else?" "Simply that one is married!" But the Housekeeper asks again, "And at night, what?" Rosita accepts the proposal joyfully as a sign of her cousin's honorable intentions. The Uncle cuts the mutable rose in his garden for the occasion. It is red now, but, he adds, "If it had to wait two hours more to be cut, I should have had to give it to you white"; and then, "But still, still it has the blush of youth." The piano is struck up again; the women dance a polka in which the Aunt and Uncle join. But there is something queer and puppet-like about the dancing figures: a strong quality of caricature, yet restrained so that the whole mood is pathetic rather than merely ludicrous:

> *Porque mujer te vi,*
> *a la orilla del mar,*
> *tu dulce languidez*
> *me hacía suspirar,*
> *y aquel dulzor sutil*
> *de mi ilusión fatal*
> *a la luz de la luna*
> *lo viste naufragar.*

> (Because I saw you, woman,
> by the shore of the sea,
> your sweet languor
> made me sigh;
> and the subtle sweetness

of my fatal illusion,
you saw in the moonlight
shipwrecked lie.)

In the third act, silence almost takes a role among the characters. The Uncle has been dead six years, and the women are now preparing to move out of the house. An empty six o'clock is striking. The whole act is heavy with desolation and the half-caught memories of those in the twilight remembering the noon-day world that has somehow slipped through their fingers. The Aunt, a rheumy broken-down thing by now, expresses this emptiness: "Some nights, coughing in my room, I hear an echo as if I were in a church." She is oppressed by her wasting life and Rosita's unfulfilled marriage to a lover who has maintained his deception by more than twenty years of false letter writing. In a violent temper, the Housekeeper would like to "grab a sword and cut his head off and smash it between two stones and cut off the hand that gave the false oath . . ." She also speaks of death, in much the same terms as Yerma and the Mother in *Bodas de Sangre*: how preferable is the knowledge of physical death, even of those close to one, to the slow death in the mind:

It is loving without finding the body; it is weeping and not knowing for whom one weeps; it is sighing for someone who one knows does not deserve it. It is an open wound endlessly trickling a tiny thread of blood, and there is nobody, nobody in the whole wide world to bring one the cotton, the bandages or the precious piece of ice.

Their last visitor is old Don Martín, who enters on a crutch. He is a dignified, sad old man, a music teacher in a fashionable academy for boys, and a frustrated poet. He speaks of the impossible pranks of the rich little brats and of the debased view people have of teachers. He recites some verses from a strongly sentimental poetic drama he has written, which the Aunt and Rosita have read several times before. The Housekeeper interrupts to bring in two workers who remove the divan "as if it were a coffin." Don Martín then speaks of a story, "Mathilda's Birthday," which he has just published in a magazine, *The Granada Mentality*. "Here I have sought to renew myself by creating something out of the modern scene. I even speak of an airplane! It's true, one has to keep up with the times." But Don Martín is called back to the academy by the news that his pupils have wrecked the plumbing and flooded the building. He takes one glorious breath before hobbling out: "I dreamed of Parnassus, and now I have to do the work of mason and plumber . . ." When the Housekeeper sees him leave, she launches on a bitter attack against the rich: "Cursed, cursed be the rich! May their nails be torn out of their fingers!" For them she constructs a fiery prison in hell, while for herself and her loved ones she pictures, in typical peasant terms, a roseate heaven resembling the florid *Purísimas* of Murillo or Cano.

Rosita enters, and the Aunt, touched by her last look on an old scene, breaks down and wails about her impractical husband and Rosita's unconsummated marriage. Rosita's own feeling, however, is restrained. She has been accustomed to living many years inside of herself and believing in illusive things. She realized her lover's inconstancy, his marriage to another long ago, in spite of his promise to her, and yet she had dream enough to live on

# WOMAN ON THE STAGE—FOLK TRAGEDIES

But it is what "people" infer and discuss that has forced her retreat inward:

> If only people had not spoken; if you had not known about it; if no one but myself had known, then his letters and his deceit would have fed my illusion, as during the first year of his absence. But everybody knew about it and I saw myself pointed out by a finger which ridiculed the modesty of my engagement and made my maiden's fan look grotesque.

She cannot ever marry now. She has made hope and love absolute entities, which she cannot modify to meet new contingencies. "Now the only thing left me is my dignity. What I have within I keep for myself alone." Emerging from her soliloquy, she is unable to abide the saddened looks of the Housekeeper and the Aunt: "Your glances of faithful dogs annoy me."

An eighteen-year-old youth enters, son of one of Rosita's old friends, María, who is now dead. The boy tells that after donning his mother's green dress he appeared so much like her that his aunt had burst into tears. Whereupon Rosita, who is much moved by the account, comments:

> There is nothing more alive than a memory. They come to make life impossible for us. That is why I understand those little old drunken women so well who go through the streets wanting to erase the world, and who sit down on the benches in the park to sing.

She is suddenly filled with this new sensitivity toward life, which allows her to look in at herself from the outside. As an impersonal observer she awakens to her own amorphous tragedy. But this is only fleeting, for she still lives within her preoccupation, which, however, will never become violent enough to wrench her from the passive abstraction of her endurance. Thus, she is not voicing the active wish but symbolizing the unattainable portion of desire when, in answer to the Aunt's forlorn words— "What we are taking are only the barest necessities: a chair to sit in and a bed to sleep in"—she replies, "To die in." Her fate, as she well knows, is botanical, the slow death of the mutable rose. When at last they leave the house, the wind rises, knocking the door shut on the garden, while outside a light drizzle begins to fall, and Rosita, taking a last look, chants the motif of the rose, ". . . and when night comes, its petals begin to fall."

*Doña Rosita la Soltera* is Lorca's most successful dramatic expression of the Granadine spirit. It triumphs in the use of a minor element, the background, which has now been invested with major dimensions. The surroundings have become a palpable force into which the lives of all the players have been infused. Transformed from a thing of light and air into a dynamo of human absorption, it takes in the essential properties of living and suffering, and throws off the fragrance of nameless, valorous generations of life. It is another version of one of Lorca's initial poetic purposes: the achievement of anonymity in an art risen from the specific locale to the universal aspect. The burden of each character in the play appears to be carried only indirectly on human shoulders; the main support is the circumambience, which keeps the tone from dropping, on the one hand, into bathos or, on the other, into full tragedy. Realizing her own suffering as an unescapable consequence of illusion, Rosita can find in it an apology for endurance which a certain sense of fanaticism or self-pity would not allow Mariana Pineda, or Yerma, or the Betrothed in *Bodas de Sangre*. Rosita is not a tragic heroine; she is only the living symbol of the mutable rose. "In the morning unfolding"—the first act—"red it is like blood"; "at noon"—the second act—"wide open and hard as coral"; when "afternoon faints . . . on the boundary line of darkness"—the third act—"it turns white, white as a cheek of salt" and "its petals begin to fall." But if Rosita will die because the present is meaningless for her (as for the Young Man in *Así Que Pasen Cinco Años*) and because ephemera cannot live in a dying form, it is the Housekeeper, we are constantly made to feel, who has become the strongest expression of the circumambience. In her is the continuity of a popular spirit which continues through the ephemerality and vicissitudes of all existence. She is the vivid red streak in the air, the strongest indelible human color in an atmosphere of botanical death.

The publication in 1946 of Lorca's suppressed drama, *La Casa de Bernarda Alba* (see APPENDIX), makes possible a summary statement regarding the poet-dramatist's use of theme in the theatre. Thus far the traditional character of his subject has been stressed. It has also been shown that esthetically his drama developed from the more subjective treatment of character and conflict noted in his experimental plays to the more objective presentation of the plight of woman in her pathetic condition of frustrated love. It is now possible to go further and show that what was implicit throughout, with *La Casa de Bernarda Alba* becomes completely manifest: that Lorca's

193

drama as a whole is an act of social criticism as well as a document of unresolved personal dilemma.

The kind of society in which woman may be made to enact a dominant role is essentially "pre-romantic." In such a society her action is functional and not sentimental. As a life-binding force her obligation as mother and matriarch is to reproduce and keep together the family group, which is still the most significant social unit. Out of such a role, and the more her function is realized in the life of the community, arise the rituals and religious taboos which ensure the continuance of the society. Whether she attends the god of the vine in his seasonal orgies or is made the repository of religious mysteries in the temple or later becomes the symbolic figure representing social virtue or man's fate, her role is always positive, preservative and undebatably integrative of society's ideals. In Spain, where the maternal and matriarchal ideals have always predominated, they have given birth to a literature of Mariolatry, feminine martyrdom, the ethical norms of the *dueña* and a castigated Donjuanism. What Lorca is saying in all his folk dramas is that the ritual which for centuries apotheosized those ideals has now succeeded in devitalizing them. What is left is a value which propels its representative to certain tragedy since it is no longer capable of being fulfilled in either personal or social terms without detriment to the individual or to society. Thus the dual failure of Mariana Pineda as a woman and the cause of freedom urged by her irresponsible love, in Lorca's first play. Thus the suicide of Adela as a fertile question and the hypocritical survival of the frigid and class-stratified answer of the mother, Bernarda Alba, in Lorca's last play. Virtue which was once a creative personal principle safeguarding in the individual the life of order against the threat of social anarchy becomes a negative abstraction and a destructive shibboleth in a society which has made it an instrument for chaos.

The personal dilemma of the poet reflected in his plays, which to some extent are the enactment of that dilemma, is precisely that of his heroines in the folk dramas: frustrated love. In personal terms lack of fulfillment suggests a conflict of sexuality through its insistence on unresolved impasse in the plays, and through it increasingly an uncontainable eroticism which *wills* the impasse.

It may be seen now why in choosing to stay close to the traditional habits of culture perception, Lorca was able to identify his dilemma with that of a society already consuming itself in its own contradictions, and why in rescuing the creative ethic which it had subdued he was able to give his theme poetic significance without strictly imaginative or dramatic resolution.

Lorca's dramatic experiments like *Mariana Pineda, Don Perlimplín, Así Que Pasen Cinco Años,* etc., all treat the problem of romantic love ironically. In *Mariana Pineda,* where the poet identifies himself with the heroine, he takes refuge with her in a martyrdom of sentimental mysticism. In *Don Perlimplín,* where he sees himself as both the erotic Belisa and her imaginative but impotent old husband, his refuge is a sadistic revenge: the creation of an imaginary young lover who betrays himself and Belisa in an act of pathetic irony. In *Así Que Pasen Cinco Años,* the cruelly materialistic heroine who rejects the Young Man for the Football Player and a car, is juxtaposed to a second-best but equally unavailing love, the Stenographer, who flees from him, while he is consoled by the voice of his imagination in the figure of an animated mannikin. His end is a half-willed suicide dictated by the card players, his own irresponsible fate.

In the folk dramas which culminate with *La Casa de Bernarda Alba,* romance no longer exists even as an ironic statement. The poet, identified with all his heroines, perpetuates desire endlessly in an eroticism which, like Yerma's, ends in a metaphysical suicide, or like Doña Rosita's, spreads itself through the fields and wells and walls of Granada's circumambience. The refuges into which all his protagonists escape are in a sense fatally predetermined by the enormity of their excessive and unfulfillable need which they realize cannot be ratified by the society and situation in which they find themselves. And they correspond, in this way, to the poet in the jail of his richly surging world of sexuality which can neither be contained without a sympathy as gigantic as his own or broken through without catastrophe. But just as the first is never encountered, so the second gradually seems, as the dénouement of play after play, more a result of the same paralyzed circumstance than a revealing resolution of a many leveled tragic insight. It is the personal dilemma which prevents Lorca's folk dramas as well as his other plays from rising so often out of pathos to real tragedy. At the same time, however, it makes for Lorca's unique sincerity as an artist and shows why a tragedy of personal validity must fail in the modern world, where it remains unresolved finally in terms of social criticism, in terms of a society which inevitably degrades as it makes meaningless personal integrity.

**196**

# 7. IMAGE INTO ACTION

THE SECRET OF LORCA'S WHOLE ART IS THAT AS A POET HE
had an overwhelming impulsion to supplement the written word by a union of various artistic media; and that
despite the consequences to which this led him, he succeeded in remaining primarily a poet. As far as it is possible to relate this endeavor to the body of work already
summarized, we may approach the virtues and defects of
his unique accomplishment.

Perhaps what at first strikes the reader curiously is that
Lorca's rich world should have been created within the
limitations of a repetitious subject matter and a simple
unchanging philosophy. Few serious modern poets dealing with the heterodox world of the present are content
to face it with so few original ideas. And most of the
ideas in Lorca's work can be found embodied in the themes
and conventions he adapted from Spanish literature. Notable in his folk plays are the insistence on themes of honor,
the defeat of innocence when seeking justification in

anarchic instinct, and the unconsummated love or marriage whose outcome is spilt blood and death. These appear in his poetry as the quest for spiritual permanence through sensual reality—a search peculiar to the Spanish temper with its mystical investment in what Unamuno has called "the tragic sense of life." If we are to question the propriety of Lorca's artistic uses as distinct from those of his contemporaries, we must examine precisely the ways in which he reshaped conventions into the dynamics of his poetry and plays. What processes were involved in his transformation from lyric poet to poetic dramatist? What advantages did he bring to the stage from his poetry, and what disadvantages? The answers to these questions should disclose Lorca's particular problem as a poet-dramatist, and by implication the problem of any modern writer interested in the function of poetry in the theatre.

Lorca's early work in poetry was concerned with the possibilities of extending imagery to include effects ordinarily found only in music and painting. One remembers vivid pictorial images: his various representations of the wind—the south wind as "swarthy" and "ardent," "bringing seeds of brilliant glances,"—the north wind as "a white bear" or as "polisher of stars"; the sky described as "full of ashes," making the fields white; children eating the moon "as if it were a plum"; the sea that "smiles from afar/ teeth of foam/ lips of sky"; or how from "behind a dirty window,/ all the children see a yellow tree/ turn suddenly into a flock of birds." There are also brief, impressionistic stanzas like statements and re-statements of a melodic theme, as in those poems of *Poema del Cante Jondo* written under titles of specific musical forms. The effort is nothing new and can most recently be identified with what the American and English Imagists were trying to do in poetry twenty-five or thirty years ago. But for Lorca this was only the beginning of an intensive experimental use which gradually led him to the rediscovery of drama as a basic poetic function.

In *Poema del Cante Jondo,* Lorca already realized the dramatic possibilities of the vignette and the episodic narrative, which are such liberal ingredients in the gypsy song and Spanish folk ballad. When this consciousness matures in *Romancero Gitano,* the drive to dramatize his imagery outruns the initial poetic function, and creates instead a whole world of character and lively conflict which become players and atmosphere for a still unwritten drama. Thus the Moon, moving her arms in the air, "shows her breasts of hard tin, shining and pure," and cautions the child not to upset her "stiffly starched whiteness"; or the wind becomes a lusting male pursuing a gypsy girl with a "warm sword"; or "an arm of night . . . a great swarthy arm with bracelets of water," or night "intimate as a little square." Again, in his depiction of three Andalusian saints in *Romancero Gitano,* Lorca's expressions are imaginative variations on conventional paintings common to the Spanish heritage of legends about saints, martyrdom, and revelations, and of all the dramatic iconography in countless provincial churches. Not only through these adaptations, but through the progressive intensification of the ballad as a dramatic instrument, Lorca finally reached the province of the stage.

In passing from the lyric-dramatic form of *Romancero Gitano* to the poetic form of his folk tragedies, he was repeating the process of dramatic adaptation as it occurred in the Golden Age. This was the transformation of the original epic into the popular ballad, and then directly into the drama, where both theme and character were continually preserved, though the literary forms had been changed. When Lorca made his gypsy the *modus vivendi* of *Romancero Gitano*, he proved that he could dramatize within a supple ballad form a well-recognized aspect of Spanish life; and in universalizing the gypsy so that the reader was able to identify himself, Lorca had found the hidden door which leads from poetry into the theatre. The same precise use of invention accompanies his entrance into the drama. For he was again transposing his subject into a recognizable traditional frame when he substituted for the silent, bronzed gypsy, agonized in his dream, the frustrated woman, agonized in her love. How realistically such a woman suited his dramatic frame is evidenced by the singular helplessness of her position as wife and lover in Catholic Spain, and by the fact that the *malcasada*, the unhappily married woman, has been a recurrent theme in all Spanish ballad literature. When she appeared in Lorca's drama, she was recognized immediately as the valiant but doomed inheritor of an already tragic role.

It will be remembered that *Mariana Pineda*, Lorca's first full-length play, followed immediately on *Romancero Gitano*, and that he called it "a popular ballad." Obviously, he was then still unsure of his powers as a dramatist, as he continued to be for some time. But he was also calling attention to the fact that his plays were experiments of a kind, which, though they were not always in poetry,

**200**

were written with the imaginative function of poetry in mind. Later, when he grew more confident of his mission in the theatre, he was willing to let a play like *Bodas de Sangre* go on the boards with the simple indication, "a tragedy." In this instance, he was supported by popular opinion, for *Bodas de Sangre* became his most universally acclaimed work. But neither it nor any of his other plays (with the possible exception of the still unpublished *La Casa de Bernarda Alba*) [1] is free from a certain fragmentariness both in the alternate use of verse and prose, and in the exclusive use of episode to the detriment of action and characterization. That such defects are real in Lorca's plays must be attributed to the frequency with which he transmuted the ballad form and his own poetic symbolism to the stage, as well as to his comparative inexperience with a box-office audience. As we have seen, he was only beginning to develop the rich possibilities of the medium in the plays he wrote immediately before his death, during a brief period of three years.

Lorca's use of musical motifs as dramatic support was another aspect of his poetry which emerged through imagery to assume a considerable part in his drama. In discussing *Así Que Pasen Cinco Años* and *Don Perlimplín*, we have implied how closely a musical esthetic is followed in the development of dramatic action. Lorca's musical knowledge was a good deal more than amateur. It is well known that Manuel de Falla once considered him his most promising pupil. Lorca arranged and composed the scores for many ballads in La Argentinita's dance repertoire, and also the music for ballads in his own plays. Federico de Onís has been working on a study of Lorca

[1] See APPENDIX.

**201**

as a folklorist composer, and there may yet exist a wide body of material to support the fact of his eminence in another field aside from poetry and drama. His musical interests certainly pervade all his literary work. Entering first into the structure of *Canciones,* a musical rather than a poetic form dominates the whole of his subsequent *Poema del Cante Jondo*—a work which can be thoroughly appreciated only through some familiarity with gypsy song, either of the *flamenco* or *cante jondo* variety. The extent to which music became more than a supplementary part of his dramatic work is clearly indicated, for example, by the strategy of dance and song in the last scene of *Yerma* which hastens and inspires the tragic denouement.

As still another esthetic complement, the ballet weaves its way into the plays. This is especially notable in sections of his "surrealist" attempts where certain characters exist only to mimic the main action of the play, as the Girl seeking her lover, who encounters the buffoons in the last act of *Así Que Pasen Cinco Años.* From the evidence of his unedited *El Público,* there is also reason to believe that the ballet form was actually to encompass the development of an entire play. Lorca also made striking use of this form in *Doña Rosita la Soltera,* which, as a period drama of darkening mood, accords with the malleable devices of song and ballet upholding all its scenes. A production of the comedy *La Zapatera Prodigiosa* has been described as "almost a ballet." His directions for introducing characters in the second act of the play would seem to indicate as much:

The *Shoemaker's Wife* is energetically wiping glasses and cups which she places on the counter. In the doorway, the *Sashmaker's*

# IMAGE INTO ACTION

*Apprentice* appears wearing his straight hat, as in the first act. He is sad. His arms hang limply and he looks at the *Shoemaker's Wife* with tenderness. The actor who in the slightest sense exaggerates this character should be struck over the head by the director. Nobody should exaggerate. The farce always exacts its own naturalness. The author has undertaken to sketch the character and the tailor to dress him. Simplicity. The *Sashmaker's Apprentice* stops in the doorway. *Don Blackbird* and the other apprentice [already seated at tables in the shoemaker's workshop, which has been transformed by his wife since his departure into a tavern] turn their heads to look at him. This takes on the appearance of a scene in a movie. The glances and expressions create the effect. The *Shoemaker's Wife* stops wiping and looks fixedly at the Apprentice. Silence.

Lorca actually composed another version of this play which was intended for ballet performance. Lola Membrives, the Argentine actress, now owns this manuscript.

In using musical and dance forms, Lorca was again keeping close to the conventions of sixteenth and seventeenth century Spanish drama with its lavish employment of supplementary devices to entertain a fickle audience. But whereas his predecessors catered mainly to the amusement-hunters (the Spanish word *pasatiempo* is in fact used to describe the drama of this period), Lorca, as the poet turned dramatic inventor and impresario, was seeking to re-educate as well as to astound a twentieth century audience grown sluggish on the prosaic fare of a "realistic" theatre. That he did not always succeed was perhaps as much due to his being the lone purveyor of a new dramatic mission as to his creating supplements which were often inadequate to the strictly theatrical requirements for dramatic action.

**203**

Finally, there is in Lorca's art the imaginative dramatization of conflict between abstract and concrete forces, developing directly from his concerns as a poet into his inventions as a dramatist. There are at least three characteristic ways in which this dramatization occurs in Lorca's imagery.

The first is as a sudden awakening of animate or inanimate things to an awareness of heightened power which is not ordinarily prescribed in their nature. All Lorca's poetry is full of such imagery; but in his later work, through continual condensation, it becomes almost a stylistic habit, which is his particular signature in contemporary poetry. Thus, in an early poem, he describes a cicada in the field: "You die drunk with light/ . . . and the sun carries off your soul/ to turn it into light"; or children singing in the meadow are "perforating the wind" with their laughter; or "battling under the weight of shadow,/ a spring ran murmuring on"; or "My head leans out/ of the window, and I see/ the knife of the wind/ yearning to cut it off." By this process, Lorca also isolates the pathos and doom inhabiting every person, place and thing separately. Thus in one poem, a horseman, riding to the city of Córdoba which he sees outlined in the distance "far off and alone," says:

> Jaca negra, luna grande,
> y aceitunas en mi alforja.
> Aunque sepa los caminos,
> yo nunca llegaré a Córdoba.

> La muerte me está mirando
> desde las torres de Córdoba.

# IMAGE INTO ACTION

> (Black pony, big moon,
> and olives in my saddlebag.
> Although I know all the roads,
> never will I reach Córdoba.
>
> . . . . .
>
> Death is gazing at me
> from the towers of Córdoba.)

In the prose fragment, *Santa Lucía y San Lázaro,* Lorca tells how "the world of grass opposed the world of minerals . . . the nail of flesh against the heart"; in *Poeta en Nueva York,* how the city sky is converted into "a hurricane of pigeons," and how "through the districts of the city sleepless people wander/ like recent survivors of a bloody shipwreck"; in *Llanto por Ignacio Sánchez Mejías,* how death "laid eggs in his wound," "the dove and the leopard are battling," and "the bull is bellowing in his forehead"; and how "Ignacio climbs the stairs/ carrying death on his shoulders." At the next step, this struggle between abstract and concrete forces suddenly breaks into the speech and action of his plays, where it explains the wild instinctual releases inviting the tragedy. In *Bodas de Sangre,* the Betrothed, speaking to the Mother, attempts to vindicate her choice of the illicit relationship with another instead of the lawful marriage with her intended Groom:

I was a woman afire, full of flame inside and out, and your son was a drop of water from whom I had hoped for children, land, prosperity; but the other was a dark river full of branches who approached me with a murmur of rushes and a song between his teeth. And I sought to run off with your son who was like a small boy of cold water, while the other promised me a hundred birds which

**205**

tripped me underfoot and left frost on my poor stained womanhood, on my girlhood embraced by fire.

More implicit in the dramatic structure, this imagistic use is even better illustrated in *Don Perlimplín,* where the old man subtly contrives to overcome by the abstract power of his imagination the sumptuous physical power of his wife's young body. He impersonates her imagined lover and then commits suicide; but though he dies, he triumphs in the fact that he has thus endowed her with a soul.

A second way in which Lorca dramatizes the conflict between abstract and concrete forces is by revealing the compulsion of one element or quality of nature to become another and throw off its own inevitable form to live vicariously in one of its own choosing. Seeking such a change of identity, for instance, are glow-worms who want to be eagles. The same occurs in the verses: "The afternoon says, I'm thirsty for shadow./ The Moon says, And I'm thirsty for morning stars./ The crystal fountain looks to the wind/ for lips and sighs"; or in "The song of water is an eternal thing./ It is light turned into song"; or in "The sea is a Lucifer of blue,/ a sky fallen for wishing to be the light." In conjunction with this is the process in which concrete things seek physical interchange through an abstract quality, such as Death in the poem of that title in *Poeta en Nueva York:* "What effort,/what an effort for the horse/ to become a dog,/what an effort for the dog to become a swallow,/ what an effort for the swallow to become a bee,/ what an effort for the bee to become a horse." When the fury of interchange is heightened, the objects in this vicarious world may become full of cannibalistic intent, as in the poem "Ruina" ("Ruin"):

# IMAGE INTO ACTION

*Detrás de la ventana,*
*con látigos y luces, se sentía*
*la lucha de la arena con el agua.*

*Yo vi llegar las hierbas*
*y les eché un cordero que balaba*
*bajo sus dentecillos y lancetas.*

. . . .

*Tú solo y yo quedamos;*
*prepara tu esqueleto para el aire.*

(With whips and lights,
the battle of sand and water
was felt behind the window.
I saw the grasses come
and threw them a lamb which bleated
under their little teeth and lancets.

. . . .

Only you and I remain;
prepare your skeleton for the wind.)

Such imagery touches the core of restless instinct in Lorca's chief dramatic characters. Thus the anxiety of Mariana Pineda is repeatedly expressed in metaphors like: "If the whole afternoon were/ like a giant bird/ how many arrows I would shoot/ to close its wings!" It also breathes in the illusion of the spinster Rosita, who would still live as she did twenty years earlier when she first began to await her lover's return, though she knows now he has long since been married to another:

I have been accustomed for many years to live outside of myself, thinking of things that were far away, and now that these things no longer exist, I still pace up and down, again and again, in a cold spot, looking for an exit I must never find.

**207**

In *Yerma,* it is voiced by the woman, her husband's impotence having doomed her to childlessness, who feels "two hammer blows" at her breasts instead of the mouth of her own child. In a larger sense, the imagery of vicarious existence approaches the theme of all Lorca's plays, turning as they do on the frustration of love, the defeat of passion, and the pathetic reaching out of hands that must return to emptiness.

The third facet of Lorca's imagistic inventions in this representation of conflict between abstract and concrete forces can be described as the achievement of a sense of halt in the rush of things forever in motion: the need of all life to find fixity, permanence, and its own endurability in rest. This is closely allied to the second process which deals with the complement of the same problem: the everlasting hunger for motion, change and illusion. Relevant here are Lorca's symbols of the mirror, the profile, the stone, and the backwater of a stream. In his early poetry we find such evidence as "I felt myself/ in a wide-openness of time./ It was a backwater/ of silence"; and "Old poplar! you've fallen/ into the mirror of the sleepy backwater"; or the description, "Every song/ is a backwater of love./ Every morning star/ a backwater/ of time,/ and every sigh,/ a backwater of the cry." Often using the legend of Narcissus, he suggests the feeling of stillness and permanence deeply underlying the cross-currents of flux: "Child, / you're going to fall in the river!/ At the bottom is a rose/ and in the rose another river./ . . . and I myself am in the rose." In *Romancero Gitano,* this sense of halt is achieved through the rigid stylization of imagery, as when "Big frozen stars/ come with the fish of shadow/ which opens the road of morning"; or when "a sky of white thighs/ closes its quicksilver eyes/ giving to the quiet penumbra/ the finality of the last heartbeat"; or through the poems of *Poeta en Nueva York,* when "All the world's light fits into one eye./ The cock sings and his song lasts longer than his wings"; when the skyline of New York is described as "profiles of lime"; when the "norm and paradise of Negroes" becomes a place where "bodies dream under the gluttony of the grass/ there, coral stones soak up the desperation of color/ the sleepers erase their profiles under the skein of snails/ and the trace of the dance remains on the last ashes." In *Llanto por Ignacio Sánchez Mejías,* Lorca approaches the full dramatic representation when he describes the spilt blood in these terms: "There is no frost of light to cool it,/ there is no song or flood of lilies,/ no crystal to cover it with silver"; or the stillness of death, in these terms: "The stone is a forehead where dreams moan,/ where there is no water bend or frozen cypresses./ . . . For the stone catches seeds and clouds,/ skeletons of larks and wolves of dark . . ."

The structural transference of this imagistic use to the stage can be illustrated again in *Don Perlimplín,* where the old husband succeeds, by suicide, in securing himself in the voluptuous rush of his wife's memory; in *Bodas de Sangre,* by the symbol of the knife, filling the Mother's talk throughout the play as a foreshadowing of doom, which appears triumphant in her last speech: with a knife/ with a tiny knife/ hardly fitting in the hand,/ but delicately penetrating/ the frightened flesh/ and stopping in the spot/ where the entangled/ root of the cry trembles." In the last act of *Así Que Pasen Cinco Años,* it occurs when the preceding action is rehearsed in the Stenographer's speech to the Young Man on a smaller stage framed within the principal stage. It is as if, in this scene, the whole meaning of the play, the consequences of an abnormal need for illusion, were frozen into a permanent flaw.

The imaginative extension of imagery into the structure of the drama emphasizes Lorca's sharply defined quest for a personal expression which would merge itself with the anonymity of folk art, a resolution to which he lent all his prodigious inventive genius. Whatever unusual device attracted him, he tried to work into the marrow of his poetry and drama. When he wandered in his "surrealist" period through a difficult and unresolved conception, he sought to distill the dramatic possibilities from his poetry for the plays which followed. Through such attempts and by transmuting the widely connotative folk emotion from the ballad into the drama, he more than once approached a resolution to the problem of poetic-dramatic integration. As any intelligent reading of his work will show, he succeeded in bringing an original dimension to his drama as a result of his accomplishment in poetry. Such a dimension, having perhaps the fault of its origin implicit in its rich expressive possibilities—that of a too literal transference of material from one medium to another—nevertheless indicated that a courageous poet working in the theatre on his own terms can still command the respect of an audience. There are few modern poets who cannot profit by the example of Lorca's tenacity of dramatic purpose, and there are few dramatists who can afford to overlook the treasure which his imaginative consistency brought to the theatre.

# 8. SIGNATURE

IF WE UNDERTAKE TO PLACE LORCA AMONG HIS CONTEMPO-
raries, we must identify him with those poets who extol
the unfathomed instincts in man as giving significance to
the life of all nature. These are the poets who, like William
Blake, would use this consciousness to deny the easy dual-
isms of mind and body, reason and emotion, intellect and
instinct. For they believe with Blake that "the body is that
part of the soul which we can see." When they accept the
world, it is a world transformed from head to foot by the
individual imagination. When they write of love, they ex-
alt sensual reality to include all forms of inanimate as well
as animate existence. Thus Whitman writes:

My lovers suffocate me,
Crowding my lips, thick in the pores of my skin,
Jostling me through streets and public halls,
Coming naked to me at night,
Crying by day *Ahoy!* from the rocks of the river, swinging and chirp-
    ing over my head,

Calling my name from flower-beds, vines, tangled underbrush,
Lighting on every moment of my life,
Bussing my body with soft balsamic kisses,
Noiselessly passing handfuls out of their hearts and giving them to
    be mine.

And in gratitude for what the earth has given him to love,
Whitman, for one, will say,

> I bequeath myself to the dirt to grow from the grass I love.
> If you want me again look for me under your boot-soles.

And Lorca, for another, in terms which are strikingly similar, will say,

> And may my blood
> on the field be sweet red mud
> where weary peasants
> may sink their spades.

This visionary identification of man as part of nature re-
lates Lorca's work to the artistic designs of modern writers
like Rimbaud, Rilke, Synge, Hardy, and D. H. Lawrence.
Like Rimbaud's *Saison en Enfer,* Lorca's *Poeta en Nueva
York* was an attempt to escape from "literature," a revolt
from a traditional poetic inheritance. Both books are a
repudiation of "verse-making"—that is, the poetry of a
fixed style, the occupation with words and images as technique. In the release of imagination both poets sought a
language purified of fetishism, and a deeper truth in the
experience of nature. Their books reflect a half-desperate,
half-playful struggle with evil and the sensation of evil.
*Saison en Enfer* and *Poeta en Nueva York* are a surrender

to death at the same time that they mark the beginning of a new life for the writers. But in the end, both books seem to contradict the original purpose: they are more obviously "literary" and fetishistic than the evidence of the poets' previous works would lead us to believe. Both show the poets captured in the steel vise of their imagination, rather than freed from it or victorious over it. Thus *Saison en Enfer* and *Poeta en Nueva York* become baffling, ingenious and profound *tours de force*. Rimbaud's denunciation of poetry was literal and complete. Lorca found himself a surer, more responsible artist in consequence of the momentary deviation. Apparently, the differences in result were owing more to complicated factors of personality than to any difference in the visionary experience.

Lorca and Rilke would seem to have more in common. Both regarded man as woman's inferior in love. Rilke went to the obscure corners of history for his allusions: to stories of passionate jilted women and to the idolatry of the Middle Ages for the Virgin. Lorca went back to the anonymous women of the folk for the leading characters of his drama. Both gave great significance to the mystic qualities of *things,* to their immanent shape and substance; and both created a personal animistic universe thereby. In the inanimate, each found embodied the pathos of life struggling against death: a whole visionary world from which the ephemera of passing human relationships were excluded. There is a striking specific basis for comparison in Rilke's *Duineser Elegien* and Lorca's *Poeta en Nueva York;* both were attempts to use language and metaphor to frame a unique experience of the human predicament. It is for both a vision of terror, in which man dwells forever in

**213**

FEDERICO GARCÍA LORCA

reach of death, without personal knowledge, without personal form, without a sense of dignity. Man knows neither heaven nor hell, but a purgatory where death begins to paralyze his marrow at the moment when life has fixed his stride. If they felt equally the tragedy of man's oblivion, they differed in that Rilke found his symbol for deep continuous consciousness in the half-human, half-divine figures of Hero and Angel, while Lorca sang of the innocent and dumb sufferers: animals, insects, flowers, children, the Negro, the Jew, the Gypsy, and everything humiliated by the gross death-touch of man.

With Synge, Lorca shares the creative mission of returning poetry to its basic dramatic function on the stage. In Lorca's work it is impossible to speak of a consistently upheld view of life. His drama celebrates the life of instinct; which is to say, it does not come bearing a message. It comes in the ancient spirit of the magician and soothsayer—to astound, to entertain, and to mystify; it also comes in the spirit of the jongleur, to invent a world and people with whose pathetically valorous lives the audience is quick to identify itself. But it has no hidden didactic motives. Synge's work is also notable for its artistic self-sufficiency, its renewal of the rich poetic language of the folk, and its re-creation of the primitive drama of feeling. Synge's comedies and tragedies dealing with the folk characters of the Irish back provinces, and especially such plays as *Riders to the Sea* and *The Playboy of the Western World,* are astonishingly close in dramatic emphasis to Lorca's *Bodas de Sangre* and to his folk comedies. They have alike the spontaneity of speech and poetic imagination which grows out of the heart of a folk untouched by

214

the perversities of city life; with whom it is still possible to express pathos and tragedy in terms of the most elemental passions. When drama reaches behind the improvised curtain of middle-class Christian morality to the lives of such people and into their wild old pagan heritage, one comes upon the springs of a new classicism in the theatre, which Synge and Lorca exemplify. But the difference is that Synge, writing in prose, accepts the conventions of the realistic theatre, and binds up his action and plot with the tight coils of traditional stage techniques. Lorca, on the other hand, a poetic dramatist reviving particular Spanish conventions on the stage and adding techniques of his own, shifts the stylistic emphasis very often from the prose speech of the characters to the verse and bright design of spectacle and musical conception. This is why Synge's theatre, temporarily at least, must be a more universally acceptable form than Lorca's.

With Hardy of the Egdon Heath novels and Lawrence of *Sons and Lovers,* we also find the instrumentality of the scene, the landscape entering into the action of life. Like Lorca, Hardy devises characters who are the rounded expressions of spontaneous instinct; full of the generosity of natural innocence, they come to grief through some imprecision of their personalities, which is constantly enlarged by the antagonism and moral outrage of the society about them. Thus with Hardy, as with Lorca, innocence finds no divine recompense; rather, innocence must nourish the germ of self-destruction in itself. Hardy, a masterly psychologist, creates complicated plots, analyzes his characters within a realistic framework, and draws leisurely philosophical analogies which accentuate his fatalistic design; Lorca, within the framework of his own poetic inventions, only hints, "Over the flower of gold, dirty sand."

Lawrence, even more clearly than Hardy or Synge, pursues the problem of frustrated love and marriage. His rebellion against the suffocating morality and social ideas arising from the Hebrew and Christian religions was an attempt to vindicate the creative instinct in man, and to find a system of values by which he could live in full dignity. After a lifetime of furious literary activity, he conceived in *The Man Who Died* the "resurrection" of Jesus as a man through an ideal mortal union with Isis, the Egyptian goddess of fecundity.

Though acutely conscious of the problem of frustrated love and its spiritual inhibitions, Lorca continued to respect the feeling for purity and form which is basic to the original Catholic morality and to the best Spanish conscience since the Golden Age. In addition, Lorca's genius was ripest as an outgrowth of Andalusian folk paganism: a world closed in on itself and sheltered from the vagrant perversities of industrial civilization. He was perhaps the last exemplar of the popular spirit which has gone out of modern poetry. Not since Whitman and Robert Burns has there been a poet who found so much of his tradition, his voice, and his instruments in his native soil. His personality and his art, which were of the same piece, appealed to a people who felt themselves incarnated in it, as in the words of the old proverb:

> *De músico, poeta y loco*
> *todos tenemos un poco.*

# SIGNATURE

(Of musician, poet and madman,
all of us have a little.)

Lorca systematically avoided the consequences of all contemporary literary heresies which resolve themselves into the private death. He stayed by the illusions of freedom and growth as they are reflected in the people living close to the land. Through such people he learned the possibility of fantasy and play which gives death the indifference it deserves, which, in fact, conquers it by accepting life as a generator, a consummation of each living moment in the fury of creative response. Ultimately his art became an answer to death in non-metaphysical terms. He saw death only as the tragedy of *sleep* bereft of the use of the senses: the cessation of man's most intimate penetration into the secret of being—sensual reality; and the thief of his most prized possession—the consciousness of a patiently hunted form in spiritual permanence. These values are real in Lorca as in practically no other modern poet, just as they must be the determinants of any poetry which hopes to outlive the catastrophes of history. For it is only the treacheries, the disloyalties of men towards these innate human values, that bring on the perversion Lorca described, and which were finally responsible for his murder.

Like many of his contemporaries, he suffered the attack upon the man of good will and the imaginative artist. But unlike the majority, he spurned voluntary exile or foreign asylum. He lived by what he conserved and loved of the Spanish people, in a world where his vision went forth, with the color of the people's blood, to sing of the life and death of the heart around the plazas and great gardens of Granada. When he died, he succumbed with the rest of Spain to the same barbarism which still hacks away at all those who are victims of the abandoned beast using their life's garden for pasturage.

# APPENDIX

IN 1945, AFTER ALMOST A DECADE OF CURIOSITY AND CONJECTURE, Lorca's play *La Casa de Bernarda Alba* was produced in Buenos Aires by Margarita Xirgu, the famous Spanish actress and the poet's close friend. In the same year a French version was staged in Paris, and later an English version in London and a Czech version in Prague. In 1946 the Spanish text was published, and in 1947 an American translation appeared. The play justifies all the anticipation aroused by earlier mention of its contents. It deserves to stand with *Bodas de Sangre* and *Yerma* as the last of the trilogy constituting Lorca's finest body of work in the theatre.

With *La Casa de Bernarda Alba,* the Lorca stage, on which women had always mounted with a certainty of their own dominance, is given over entirely to their propriety. No male character is seen throughout the play. But this is not the only way in which it is distinguished from the other plays. In an introductory note to *Bernarda*, Lorca states that "these three acts are intended to be a documentary photograph." It has been noted how Lorca's drama from *Bodas de Sangre* to *Doña Rosita* and *Yerma* was tending in structure and characterization toward a more realistic, a less poetically intrusive line of development. In this sense *Bernarda* is the only Lorca play in which exposition, complication, movement and climax are dramatically self-determined: determined, that is, by the strict necessity of character and situation, and not by any auxiliary

**219**

concerns for supernatural, pictorial, musical or dance effects. Even the exclusion of male characters from the stage is not the tour de force it might at first seem: it proceeds from the nature of the dramatic situation and from the character of Bernarda in her tyranny over the lives of those about her.

The first act opens on the interior of "a very white room in Bernarda Alba's house," where the whiteness of the walls and the arched doorways, the blank silent atmosphere of enclosure, and the dim sound of bells tolling outside suggest the interior of an egg. (Whiteness is a major motif in the play: from the whiteness of the walls, the whiteness of embroidered linen and sheets to the tragic whiteness of virginity, with which reference the play ends. Even the name *Alba*, whose meaning is *dawn* or *daylight*, is derived from the Latin word for *white*.) The first characters to appear are Poncia, general household servant, and her assistant, a maid. We learn that Bernarda and her daughters are attending the funeral of the master of the house. We also learn of Bernarda's savage miserliness, her tyranny over daughters and servants, and her sanctimoniousness. Like all of Lorca's peasant characters, Poncia is a richly human creature. More than other such characters, however, she is conscious of Bernarda's ingratitude and overwhelming class prejudice. The attitude of both servants—deep resentment at their own ill-treatment and a resignation tinged with bitterness in the knowledge of Bernarda's husband's death—is revealed in the lament of Poncia's helper just before Bernarda, her daughters, and the group of female mourners enter the house: "Bring on the coffin with its golden borders and the brocade to carry it on—because what happens to you will happen to me too! Don't let it bother you—Antonio Maria Benavides, stiff in your woolen suit and your high boots! Don't let it bother you! Now you'll never come again to lift my petticoats behind the stable door!"

The servant's semi-hysteria is broken by the dry disdain of Bernarda's entrance, when she remarks about her: "The poor are like animals; they seem made of different stuff." In the woman-crammed room, lemonade is served amid the bated gossip about the men seen at church. At one point Bernarda venomously interjects: "In church women shouldn't look at any man but the priest, and at him because he wears skirts. Turning your head is to be looking for the warmth of corduroy."

After the mourners depart, Bernarda's maledictions follow them. She now promises not only to keep out future visitors but to seal her daughters in the house for "eight years of mourning," while they embroider their hope-chest linen. Adela, the youngest daughter, who is twenty, reports that Angustias, the eldest, who is thirty-nine, was looking through a crack in the door at the men leaving the patio, and was listening to their conversation. Bernarda calls for Angustias and strikes her. Then she orders all the girls to leave the room while she questions Poncia intently about the men's conversation. Poncia tells her about "the only bad woman" in the village who was happily carried off the previous night by a group of reapers who had managed to tie up her husband first. They had all taken their pleasure with her— "They say she rode with her breasts showing and Maximiliano took her and held her as though he were playing a guitar."

When Bernarda and Poncia leave the stage, the two daughters, Martirio, twenty-four, and Amelia, twenty-seven, enter. Martirio, as her name suggests, has adopted a fatalistic attitude. She points out how her aunt Adelaide has suffered because of men, how she herself has feared men since childhood, and how glad she is for her own ugliness which has kept suitors from her. Magdalena, who is thirty, joins them to tell of Pepe el Romano's courtship of Angustias. He is a young man of twenty-five who, though naturally disposed to Adela because of her spirit and youth, wants Angustias because she has inherited all her father's money. When Adela enters and hears about Pepe and Angustias, her spirits fall and she shouts out her rebelliousness. A servant announces that Pepe may be seen from a window passing along the streets; they all rush upstairs to watch him. The act closes with the wild entrance of Maria Josefa, Bernarda's eighty-year-old mother, who has inexplicably escaped from the room where Bernarda had kept her locked during the funeral. Decked in gay flowers, she demands her mantilla and her necklace of pearls, because she wants to marry a virile young man by the seashore. Her final cry is not a muddled statement, but one that fixes the situation of the play firmly and sanely: "I don't want to watch these old maids, dying to get married, grinding their hearts to dust. I want to return to my village. Bernarda, I want to marry a strong young man and to be happy with him." At Bernarda's command, they all seize the grandmother and drag her offstage.

In the second act, there is the growing sense that a good many wild significant things are happening offstage: that, in fact, just as the sickness and violence in all the characters is inward and repressed, so the real drama, in the numerous sallies of lusty men, the gossip of townspeople, the lurking presence of Pepe, the furious kicking of the stallion against the stable doors, is invading from offstage somewhere the teetering egg, the white jail of the visible stage.

Bernarda's daughters and Poncia are sewing and embroidering. They speak in short subdued phrases, and seem in the heavy quiet which surrounds them to be working on their shrouds instead of their wedding sheets. The forthcoming marriage between Angustias and Pepe is accepted by all except Adela, who is said to be in her bedroom. A sense of violent expectancy is aroused by Poncia's hint that although Pepe, who has been courting Angustias under her window, was understood to have left her at one the previous night, Poncia herself heard him leave at four. With hearty freedom, Poncia expands on the subject of her own memories of courtship days. Later, after the others have gone out, Poncia confronts Adela, and asks her: "Why did you stand half naked at the open window, with the lights on, when Pepe went by on the second night to talk to your sister?" She urges Adela not to defame God's law, but to endure the short months that will pass after Pepe marries Angustias, until the latter dies in childbirth, as she inevitably must, because she is sickly and "narrow-waisted." Then Pepe will do what all rich widowers do: he will marry her, Adela, the youngest and prettiest of the daughters. Adela disdains Poncia's advice and insists she will do what she pleases with her body. The others return to their sewing and hear Poncia's story of a recent seduction of a dancer in the village by the reapers, "forty or fifty handsome young men." The air grows heavier; outside the song of the reapers is heard as they go off to the fields. As the song fades, Martirio and Adela softly repeat the last verses. Now Angustias "bursts in furiously, in a way that contrasts greatly with the previous silence," accusing her sisters of having stolen her framed photograph of Pepe. None will admit it, though suspicion is cast upon Adela. But Poncia goes out and soon returns with the photograph which she found hidden between Martirio's bedsheets. When Bernarda towers over Martirio, Angustias restrains her mother. Martirio explains that it was all a joke. Adela, now alive to a real rivalry, bitterly denounces Martirio for her hypocrisy. Bernarda violently promises to chain her daughters in "this house my father built"; and then she orders them out, beating her cane on the floor.

In the conversation which ensues between Poncia and Bernarda on what Poncia calls the impending "grave danger," Bernarda ruthlessly assails her servant, insulting Poncia's mother and her trashy origin. In turn Poncia tells Bernarda that after seeing Angustias the night before, Pepe is known to have entertained himself at the window of one of the other daughters. Now, just as the girls enter, a great commotion arises in the street outside. Everybody rushes out but Adela and Martirio, and in a scene of uncontainable emotion, the former admits having received Pepe the night before; now Martirio vows to tear him out of her arms. The tumult outside increases, and a servant enters with the news that an unmarried girl is being dragged through the streets because she "had a child and no one knows whose it is." Bernarda approves the scene and loudly urges the populace to kill the girl by putting "hot coals in the place where she sinned." At this, in pity and terror, Adela places her hands over her belly, crying "No! No!" when the curtain falls.

In the final act, the suppressed restlessness which leads to the dénouement of the play is introduced in Bernarda's solemn conversation with a neighbor, Prudencia, who is going blind. The five daughters sit about eating while Angustias' approaching marriage is discussed perfunctorily by the two older women. The noise of a stallion hammering with his hooves at the stable door twice interrupts the talk. When Prudencia leaves, Adela gets up to walk about the patio and is immediately followed by Amelia and Martirio. Bernarda has chosen to ignore the conflict among her daughters because any recognition of it would offend her pride. When the three girls return, it is only to report the thick standing darkness of the night outside in which, as Adela puts it, the stallion could be seen "in the middle of the corral, white, twice as large, filling the whole darkness." With the news that Pepe is not expected to come that night, the daughters leave for bed. Soon after Bernarda goes to bed, Adela appears in her petticoat, pretending to want a drink of water. As she goes out, Maria Josefa appears on the stage again, holding a lamb in her arms and singing to it as though it were her child, while she finds place in her song for defamatory verses about "Bernarda, old leopard-face," and "Magdalena, hyena face." Martirio enters to watch Adela near the corral door and is met by the grandmother who, in the closet of her madness, is still luminous with insight concerning the situation in the house: "Pepe is a giant, and all of you love him. But he's going to devour you because you are grains of wheat. Not grains of wheat. Frogs without tongues!" After Martirio locks her up, she calls to Adela, who tells her that she, Adela, is ready to be Pepe's mistress. Martirio, who also admits her love for Pepe, vows never to allow Adela to have him. A whistle is heard outside and Adela runs to the door, but Martirio bars the way. In the struggle which ensues, Martirio manages to arouse her mother, and points out Adela's disgrace. While all the other women enter, Bernarda goes for her rifle, reappears with it, and leaves the stage. A shot is heard, which Martirio deliberately misinterprets to Adela as the shot which has killed her lover. Adela goes to her room. Actually Bernarda's aim was faulty, and by now Pepe is safe on his horse galloping among the trees. A thud is heard in Adela's room. Poncia breaks the door in and finds that the youngest daughter has killed herself. Solemnly, fanatically, Bernarda takes the situation in hand, exclaiming, "My daughter died a virgin. Carry her to her bed and dress her as though she were a virgin. Say nothing about this to anyone. She died a virgin. At dawn, let it be known so that the bells will be rung twice."

Bernarda is the symbol and heroine of the play—not Poncia or any of the daughters. More symbol than person, she obtrudes painfully and irremediably on the reader's consciousness, more so than any character in any other Lorca play. She is not consumed by the tragedy; she consumes it. It would be easy to identify her as an incarnation of evil, but one ought to be prepared to say first of

**224**

what evil she is the body. I do not know how final or how valid an explanation of that evil can be demonstrated. Most obviously she is a force of repression which survives behind various masks: that of family pride, that of inverted traditional honor, and that of religious piety. But since the reader of the play does not mistake her as sincerely representing any of these (her name, in fact, would signify as much—*prevarication, false boast*), her action as the represser of the life force becomes the most feasible means of identifying her.

In another sense, she is the perpetuation of the principle of sterility which concerned Lorca in *Yerma* and in *Así Que Pasen Cinco Años*—part of the unresolvable personal conflict which has been noted in all his work. Bernarda also represents another part of the circumambience which Lorca was always celebrating; but now it is that Spain in its little jail of localism, of narrow and traditional intolerance, which literally consumed the poet himself. The alleviating forces of warm sentiment and peasant vigor which were permitted in his other plays have turned into a senile madness (Maria Josefa) and a bitter sense of social recrimination (Poncia) in *La Casa de Bernarda Alba*.

The symbolism of the play is further extended in the case of the five daughters. In Adela, in whom the life force is strongest, there is something of the same struggle against fate and stoicism which we find in Yerma. But Adela's situation allows for no moral code like Yerma's; her struggle is anarchic and self-destructive. In none of the daughters, in fact, is there any indication of integral moral beauty. Angustias, as her name suggests, is full of affliction and anguish; her wealth gives her some advantage over the other daughters, but she is physically and morally on her last legs. Martirio has taken refuge in a sense of martyrdom, which because of her unreciprocated love for Pepe fits her badly, hypocritically. Magdalena is the least hopeful of all and the most humble; for that reason she comes closest to being reconciled to her situation, though if she does her reconciliation is without principle. Amelia is the least definite of the daughters; she hovers between Martirio and Adela, without, however, finding a pattern of action of her own. As is implied in the subtitle of the play—"A Drama About

**225**

Women in the Villages of Spain"—the daughters are intended more as representatives of general feminine attitudes than as persons in a real family group. Thus, toward the end of the last act, Martirio's vindictive outburst against Adela may be understood as an illustration of this intention: "Don't embrace me! Don't try to smooth this over. My blood is no longer yours. Though I might try to look at you as my sister, I can't take you as anything more than just another woman."

Just as the play would seem to belong with *Yerma* and *Bodas de Sangre* as the last of a dramatic trilogy, so it seems also to give— even as Lorca's most objective dramatic work, his most impersonal and non-poetic—the final thematic definition of the poet's own problem, and to anticipate the condition of Spain on the verge of its self-destruction. Without claiming for the play any specific political intention, what could now be clearer than that the painfully destructive tradition which Bernarda perpetuates through the victimization of her daughters belongs to the triumph of those forces which pushed hope and dignity out of Spain and almost out of the world?

# SELECTED BIBLIOGRAPHY

(The fullest García Lorca bibliography to date is included in the *Obras Completas*, Aguilar, 1960. Although superseding Sidonia C. Rosenbaum's earlier listings in *Federico García Lorca (1899–1936)*, Hispanic Institute of the United States, N.Y., 1941, the Aguilar bibliography is far from being complete. Its listings for the Slavic languages are scanty (Lorca's plays are widely published in Poland, Czechoslovakia, Russia, Yugoslavia); Italian and Scandinavian references are meagre, and entries in French and English are barely adequate.)

## I. FEDERICO GARCÍA LORCA

### 1. Books

*Obras Completas,* ed. Arturo del Hoyo, pról. Jorge Guillén, epíl. Vicente Aleixandre, 4a edición, Aguilar, Madrid, 1960.
   (Main titles are: PROSA: *Impresiones* (1918); *Narraciones; Conferencias; Homenajes.* POESÍA: *Libro de Poemas* (1921); *Poema del Cante Jondo* (1921); *Primeras Canciones* (1922); *Canciones* (1921–1924); *Romancero Gitano* (1924–1927); *Poeta en Nueva York* (1929–1930); *Llanto por Ignacio Sánchez Mejías* (1935); *Seis Poemas Galegos* (1935); *Diván*

*del Tamarit* (1936); *Poemas Sueltos; Cantares Populares.*
TEATRO: *El Maleficio de la Mariposa* (1919); *Los Títeres
de Cachiporra: Tragicomedia de Don Cristóbal y la Seña
Rosita; Mariana Pineda* (1925); *Teatro Breve* (1928); *La Zapatera Prodigiosa* (1930); *Amor de Don Perlimplín con Belisa
en su Jardín* (1931); *Retablillo de Don Cristóbal* (1931); *Así
Que Pasen Cinco Años* (1931); *El Público* /two scenes/
(1933); *Bodas de Sangre* (1933); *Yerma* (1934); *Doña Rosita
la Soltera, o El Lenguaje de las Flores* (1935); *La Casa de
Bernarda Alba* (1936). OTRAS PÁGINAS: *Impresiones y
Paisajes* /selections/ (1918). VARIA: *Impresiones; Narra-
ciones; Conferencias; Artículos; Cartas de FGL; Entrevistas y
Declaraciones; Poesías.* APÉNDICE: *Dibujos y Música de las
Canciones de FGL.* CRONOLOGÍA DE LA VIDA Y DE LA
OBRA DE FGL. BIBLIOGRAFÍA: I Ediciones; II Traduc-
ciones; III Estudios y Homenajes; IV Sobre Nuestra Edición.
NOTAS AL TEXTO.)

*Obras Completas,* ed Guillermo de Torre, vols. 1–8, Edit. Losada,
Buenos Aires, 1936–1946.

*Cartas a Sus Amigos,* con un prólogo de Sebastián Gasch, Ediciones Cobalto, Barcelona, 1950. (Letters to Sebastián Gasch,
Guillermo de Torre, Ana María Dalí, Ángel Ferrant, and Juan
Guerrero; reproductions of thirty photographs, letters and
drawings.)

*Dibujos de García Lorca* (Lorca's Drawings), introd. Gregorio
Prieto, Colección de la Cariatide I, Afrodisio Aguado, Madrid,
1949. (bilingual text)

*Impresiones y Paisajes,* Tipografía P. V. Traveset, Granada, 1918.
(Only part included in Aguilar *Obras Completas;* out of print.)

*Canciones del Teatro de Federico García Lorca,* edited by Gustavo
Pittaluga, Union Musical Española, Madrid, 1960.

## 2. In Translation

### a) Collections

*Five Plays: Comedies and Tragicomedies,* tr. James Graham-Lujan
and Richard L. O'Connell, New Directions, Norfolk, 1963.

# BIBLIOGRAPHY

*From Lorca's Theatre: Five Plays of Federico García Lorca,* trans. Richard L. O'Connell & James Graham-Lujan, Scribner's, N.Y., 1941.

*Lament for the Death of a Bullfighter and Other Poems,* tr. A. L. Lloyd, Oxford University Press, N.Y., 1937; Heinemann, London, 1953. (bilingual text)

*Lorca: Gypsy Ballads,* tr. Langston Hughes, *Beloit Poetry Journal Chapbook No. 1,* Beloit, 1951.

*Poems,* tr. Stephen Spender & J. L. Gili, introd. R. M. Nadal, Oxford University Press, N.Y., 1939.

*Poet in New York,* tr. and ed. Ben Belitt, introd. Ángel del Río, Grove Press, N.Y., 1955. (Contains complete and accurate text, bilingual; appendices with relevant poems and prose, and two Lorca lectures: "The *Duende:* Theory and Divertissement," and "The Poetic Image of Don Luis de Góngora".)

*Poet in New York and Other Poems,* tr. Rolfe Humphries, W. W. Norton, N.Y., 1940.

*Selected Poems,* ed. Francisco García Lorca and Donald M. Allen, New Directions (The New Classics Series #36), Norfolk, 1955; (New Directions Paperbook #114) 1962.

*Some Little-Known Writings of Federico García Lorca,* tr. and introd. Edwin Honig, *New Directions No. 8,* New Directions, Norfolk, 1944.

*The Gypsy Ballads,* tr. Rolfe Humphries, Indiana University Press, Bloomington, 1953.

*Three Tragedies,* tr. James Graham-Lujan & Richard L. O'Connell, introd. Francisco García Lorca, New Directions, N.Y., 1947.

## b) Plays, Lectures, Major Poems

*Billy-Club Puppets, Tragicomedy of Don Cristóbal* (See *Five Plays: Comedies and Tragicomedies*).

*Bitter Oleander* (*Bodas de Sangre* adapted), tr. José A. Weissman (MS), New York Public Library, N.Y., 1935.

*Blood Wedding,* tr. William I. Oliver (MS microfilm), Columbia University Library, N.Y., 1957.

*Blood Wedding,* tr. Gilbert Neiman, *New Directions No. 4,* New Directions, Norfolk, 1939.

**229**

*Blood Wedding,* tr. Graham-Lujan & O'Connell (see *Three Trage-dies*).

*Buster Keaton's Constitutional,* tr. William I. Oliver (MS micro-film), Columbia University Library, N.Y., 1957.

*Buster Keaton's Promenade,* tr. Tim Reynolds, *Accent,* Summer, 1957.

*The Butterfly's Evil Spell,* tr. James Graham-Lujan and Richard L. O'Connell (see *Five Plays: Comedies and Tragicom-edies*).

*Chimera,* tr. Edwin Honig (see *Some Little-Known Writings*).

*Chimera,* tr. Tim Reynolds, *Accent,* Summer, 1957.

*Dialogue of Amargo,* tr. Edwin Honig (see *Some Little-Known Writings*).

*Episode of the Lieutenant Colonel of the Civil Guard,* tr. Edwin Honig (see *Some Little-Known Writings*).

*Doña Rosita, the Spinster,* tr. Graham-Lujan & O'Connell (see *From Lorca's Theatre* and *Five Plays: Comedies and Tragi-comedies*).

*Gypsy Ballads* (six), tr. A. L. Lloyd (see *Lament*).

*Gypsy Ballads* (twelve), tr. Roy Campbell (see *Campbell's Lorca*).

*Gypsy Ballads* (twelve), tr. in prose, J. L. Gili (see *Lorca*).

*If Five Years Pass,* tr. Graham-Lujan & O'Connell (see *From Lorca's Theatre*).

*In the Frame of Don Cristóbal,* tr. Edwin Honig (see *Some Little-Known Writings*).

*Lament for Ignacio Sánchez Mejías* (excerpts), tr. Roy Campbell (see *Campbell's Lorca*).

*Lament for Ignacio Sánchez Mejías,* tr. A. S. Ferguson, *The Aberdeen University Review,* XXVI, 1939.

*Lament for Ignacio Sánchez Mejías,* tr. in prose, J. L. Gili (see *Lorca*).

*Lament for Ignacio Sánchez Mejías,* tr. J. L. Gili and Stephen Spender (see *Poems*).

*Lament for Ignacio Sánchez Mejías,* tr. Lloyd Mallan, *Southern Review,* VI, 1941.

*Lament for the Death of a Bullfighter,* tr. Warren Carrier, *Read-*

# BIBLIOGRAPHY

*ing Modern Poetry*, ed. Engle & Carrier, Scott, Foresman Co., N.Y., 1955.

*Lorca, Selected and Translated*, J. L. Gili, Penguin Poets (D51), England, 1960. (Bilingual, poems with prose translations.)

*Mariana Pineda*, tr. James Graham-Lujan. *Tulane Drama Review*, Vol. 7, No. 2. Winter 1962.

*Santa Lucía and San Lázaro*, tr. Edwin Honig (see *Some Little-Known Writings*).

*The Audience* /two scenes/, tr. Ben Belitt, *Evergreen Review No. 6*, Grove Press, N.Y., 1958.

*The Divan at the Tamarit*, tr. Edwin Honig (see *Some Little-Known Writings*).

*The Divan del Tamarit* /in part/, tr. W. S. Merwin, Edwin Honig, Stephen Spender (see *Selected Poems*).

"The *Duende*: Theory and Divertissement," tr. Ben Belitt (see *Poet in New York*).

*The House of Bernard Alba*, tr. Graham-Lujan & O'Connell (see *Three Tragedies*).

*The Lass, the Sailor and the Student*, tr. William I. Oliver (MS microfilm), Columbia University Library, N.Y., 1957.

*The Love of Don Perlimplín for Belisa in His Garden*, tr. Graham-Lujan & O'Connell (see *From Lorca's Theatre* and *Five Plays: Comedies and Tragicomedies*).

*The Marvellous Shoemaker's Wife*, tr. Roy Campbell (MS microfilm), Columbia University Library, N.Y.

"The Poetic Image in Don Luis de Góngora," tr. Ben Belitt (see *Poet in New* York).

"Theory and Function of the *Duende*," tr. J. L. Gili (see *Lorca, Selected and Translated* by Gili).

*The Shoemaker's Prodigious Wife*, tr. Graham-Lujan & O'Connell (see *From Lorca's Theatre* and *Five Plays: Comedies and Tragicomedies*).

*The Spell of the Butterfly*, tr. William I. Oliver (MS microfilm), Columbia University Library, N.Y., 1957.

*The Tragicomedy of Don Cristobita and Doña Rosita*, tr. William I. Oliver, *New World Writing No. 8*, New American Library of World Literature, N.Y., 1955.

*The Virgin, the Sailor and the Student,* tr. Tim Reynolds, *Accent,* Summer, 1957.

*Yerma,* tr. Graham-Lujan & O'Connell (see *Three Tragedies*).

## II. SECONDARY STUDIES

### 1. Books

Babin, María Teresa. *Federico García Lorca: Vida y obra,* Las Americas, New York, 1955.

Barea, Arturo. *Lorca, the Poet and the People,* Harcourt Brace, New York, 1949.

Berenguer Carisomo, Arturo. *Las máscaras de Federico García Lorca,* Talleres gráficos, Buenos Aires, 1941.

Correa, Gustavo. *La poesía mítica de Federico García Lorca,* University of Oregon Publications, Eugene, 1957.

Crow, John. *Federico García Lorca,* University of California, Los Angeles, 1945.

Díaz-Plaja, Guillermo. *Federico García Lorca: Estudio crítico,* Espasa Calpe, Buenos Aires, 1954.

Campbell, Roy. *Lorca, an Appreciation of his Poetry,* Yale University Press, New Haven, 1952.

Eich, Christoph. *Federico García Lorca: Poeta de la intensidad,* Edit. Gredos, Madrid, 1958.

Flecniakoska, Jean-Louis. *L'Universe Poétique de Federico García Lorca,* Bordeaux-Paris, Edit. Bière, 1952.

Flys, Jaroslaw M. *El lenguaje poético de Federico García Lorca,* Edit. Gredos, Madrid, 1955.

García-Luengo, Eusebio. *Revisión del teatro de Federico García Lorca,* Política y literatura cuaderno, núm. 3, Artes gráficas, Madrid, 1951.

Gebser, Jean. *Lorca, oder Das Reich der Mütter,* Deutsche Verlags-Anstalt, Stuttgart, 1949.

Guardia, Alfredo de la. *Federico García Lorca, persona y creación,* Schapere, Buenos Aires, 1944.

Guillén, Jorge. *Federico en persona: Semblanza en epistolario,* Emecé Edit., Buenos Aires, 1959.

# BIBLIOGRAPHY

Machado Bonet, Ofelia. *Federico García Lorca. Su producción dramática,* Impresa Rosgal, Montevideo, 1951.

Morla Lynch, Carlos. *En España con Federico García Lorca (páginas de un diario íntimo, 1928–1936),* Aguilar, Madrid, 1957; rev. ed., 1958.

Nourissier, François. *Federico García Lorca: Dramaturge* (Les Grands Dramaturges), L'Arche Edit., 3, Paris, 1955.

Parrot, Louis. *Federico García Lorca,* Seghers (Coll. des poetes d'aujourd'hui), Paris, 1949.

Río, Ángel del. *Vida y obras de Federico García Lorca,* Heraldo de Aragón, Zaragoza, 1952.

Robles, Emmanuel. *García Lorca,* Edit. du Cactus, Algier, 1949.

Mora Guarnido, José. *Federico García Lorca y su mundo,* Losada, Buenos Aires, 1958.

Sánchez, Roberto G. *García Lorca: Estudio sobre su teatro,* Ediciones Jura, Madrid, 1950.

Schonberg, Jean-Louis. *Federico García Lorca: L'homme, l'oeuvre,* Librairie Plon, Paris, 1956.

Trend, J. B. *Lorca and the Spanish Poetic Tradition,* Basil Blackwell, Oxford, 1956.

Vásquez Ocaña, Fernando. *García Lorca, vida, cántico y muerte,* Grijalbo, México, 1957.

Vian, Cesco. *Federico García Lorca, poeta e dramaturgo,* Universita Cattolica, Milan, 1951.

## 2. Articles

Bentley, Eric. "The Poet in Dublin" (on staging *The House of Bernarda Alba*), *In Search of Theatre,* pp. 215–232, Alfred A. Knopf, New York, 1953.

Brenan, Gerald. "Granada" (on Lorca's death), *The Face of Spain,* pp. 131–160, Grove Press, New York, 1956.

Fergusson, Francis. "Don Perlimplín: Lorca's Theatre-Poetry," *Kenyon Review,* XVII, pp. 337–348, Spring, 1955.

García Lorca, Francisco. Prologue to *Three Tragedies of Federico García Lorca,* New Directions, New York, 1947.

**233**

García Lorca, Francisco. "Yerma dans l'oeuvre de Federico García Lorca," *L'Avant-Scene, Paris,* no. 98, 1954.

Helman, Edith F. Introduction, Spanish text edition of *La zapatera prodigiosa,* W. W. Norton, New York, 1952.

Jiménez, Juan Ramón. "Crisis del espíritu en la poesía española," *Nosotros,* V, nos. 46 & 49, pp. 165–182, marzo-abril 1940.

Kelin, F. "On Lorca in Russian," *International Literature,* II, pp. 50–55, Moscow, 1943.

López-Morillas, Juan. "García Lorca y el primitivismo lírico: Reflexiones sobre el *Romancero gitano,*" *Intelectuales y espirituales,* pp. 195–216, Revista de Occidente, Madrid, 1961.

Martínez Nadal, R. Introduction to Lorca's *Poems* (tr. Spender and Gili), Oxford University Press, New York, 1939.

Morby, E. S. "García Lorca in Sweden," *Hispanic Review,* XIV, pp. 38–46.

Nims, John Frederick. Explications of five Lorca poems (*Preciosa y el aire; Romance somnámbulo; La casada infiel; Romance de la pena negra; Despedida*), *The Poem Itself* (ed. Stanley Burnshaw), Holt, Rinehart and Winston, New York, 1960.

Pérez Marchand, M. L. "La inquietud existencial en la poesía de Federico García Lorca," *Asomante* (San Juan, P.R.), V, 1949, pp. 72–86.

Riley, Edward C. "Considerations on the Poetry of García Lorca," *The Dublin Magazine,* no. 2, 1952, pp. 14–22.

Salinas, Pedro. "Dramatismo y teatro de Federico García Lorca," *Literatura española del siglo xx,* Séneca, México, 1941, pp. 289–302.

Salinas, Pedro. "Lorca and the Poetry of Death," *Hopkins Review,* V, pp. 5–12.

Williams, William Carlos. "Federico García Lorca," *Kenyon Review,* I, 1939, pp. 148–155.

Zardoya, Concha. "La técnica metafórica de Federico García Lorca," *Revista Hispánica Moderna,* XX, 1944, New York.

# INDEX

**235**

# INDEX

**EDWIN HONIG** was born in New York City in 1919; he studied at Columbia, the University of Michigan, and the University of Wisconsin, where he took two degrees. After employment at the Library of Congress, he served in the U.S. Army in Europe during the Second World War. He has taught at New York University, Illinois Institute of Technology, Purdue, the University of New Mexico, the University of Wisconsin, Claremont College, and Harvard, where he was Briggs-Copeland Assistant Professor of English.

He is a poet (*The Moral Circus* and *The Gazabos: 41 Poems*), the author of the critical study, *Dark Conceit: the Making of Allegory*, a translator (*Calderón: Four Plays* and *Cervantes: Eight Interludes*), and co-editor of *The Mentor Book of Major American Poets*. Since 1940 he has contributed verse, essays, fiction, and translations to numerous magazines, including *The Kenyon Review*, *Sewanee Review*, *The Nation*, *Saturday Review*, *San Francisco Review*, *Poetry*, *Tulane Drama Review*, *New Mexico Quarterly*, *Southwest Review*, the *Massachusetts Review*, and the *Virginia Quarterly Review*.

In 1961 he received the Golden Rose Award of the New England Poetry Club, and has twice held a Guggenheim fellowship. At present he is Professor of English at Brown University.